MACARONS

Math, Science, and Art
for the mathematically challenged, non-scientific novice

By
Paula A.L. Quinene
Exercise Scientist & Pastry-Chef-at-Heart

Copyright © 2013 by Paula Ann Lujan Quinene

ISBN 978-0-7414-9613-3 Paperback
ISBN 978-0-7414-9614-0 eBook
Library of Congress Control Number: 2013907801

Printed in the United States of America

Published June 2013

INFINITY PUBLISHING
1094 New DeHaven Street, Suite 100
West Conshohocken, PA 19428-2713
Toll-free (877) BUY BOOK
Local Phone (610) 941-9999
Fax (610) 941-9959
Info@buybooksontheweb.com
www.buybooksontheweb.com

TABLE OF CONTENTS

TABLE OF FIGURES

ACKNOWLEDGEMENTS

My husband has been a trooper in accepting a few missed lunches and some not-so-fancy dinners since I began my unexpected quest into macaron la-la land. Thanks a bunch Nen.

More than I can ever give back to you Mom, thank you for teaching-by-doing, for many things including how to decorate cakes.

For my Facebook fans, much appreciation for all your encouragement and support.

To my editor Laura Carlson, of American Editing Services, thank you so much for your fantastic help. Laura may be contacted via americaneditingservices.com.

INTRODUCTION

Macaron Cookies

Modern macaron—ma-ka-rohn—cookies, not to be confused with coconut macaroons, are basically two discs of nutty meringue that sandwich a filling. I distinguish between the single macaron discs—macarons or macs—and the completely assembled macaron cookies because the macaron discs are unfilled and not quite ready to eat, while the macaron cookies are a treat that require a few more steps. Coconut macaroons, on the other hand, are singular mounds of cookies made of liquid egg whites, sugar, and coconut.

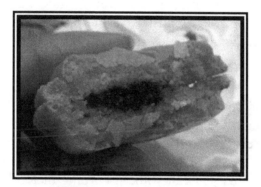

Figure 1 - Raspberry macaron from A Southern Season in Chapel Hill, NC

Meringue

A meringue is mostly egg whites whipped with granulated sugar. Stabilizers such as cream of tartar, meringue powder, egg white powder, and starch may also be added; some recipes include salt. Meringue is used to lighten and add volume to many sweet goodies, including cakes, icings, soufflés, mouse, and cookies. Meringue may be served as a topping such as in meringue pies or baked Alaska's. Meringue may also be prepared as containers for fruits and cooked fillings.

There are three methods of making the meringue that are used for macaron discs. Swiss meringue entails heating egg whites with sugar then whipping the mixture. Italian meringue requires that you add hot sugar syrup to the egg whites that are still being whipped. French meringue, also called basic meringue, is the least time-consuming, though most delicate style of making meringue; it blends sugar into room temperature egg whites. The basic meringue method of preparing macarons is the focus of this book. Meringue is the "wet" component of the macaron batter.

Macaronage

A mixture of ground nuts and powdered sugar is combined with the meringue—a process referred to as macaronage—to produce a firm, yet flowing macaron batter. This technique enables the tip of the piped batter to disappear into the surrounding batter. Additionally, macaronage deflates some of the air bubbles so that the discs don't expand too much.

Oven Heat

The heat in the oven sets the structure of the meringue and gives the macarons their characteristic feet. The amount of heat and the rate of heat application are vital for perfect macarons, and these can potentially be the most unstable aspect of making macarons. Without a convection oven, you must create an extremely stable meringue and quickly apply as much constant heat to your cookies as you can without burning them. The heat creates the feet and holds the meringue in place so the macarons don't become hollow.

Moving Forward

The intent of this book is to make the process of creating beautiful and hollow-free macaron cookies as painless, as efficient, and as gratifying as possible—using math and science. The book begins with a sprinkling of academics before venturing into the key aspect of making macarons—the heat from a gas, an electric, and a convection oven. Next, I'll explain the changes you can make to your technique and the tools needed if you are not using a convection oven. Thereafter, I'll go into the science of the ingredients used in making macarons. I'll walk you through my macaron experiments where you will see the painstaking efforts it took to get to the "perfect" macaron recipe. Finally, I'll share my recipes for the discs and the fillings.

Most major headings in this book have a "Results and Recommendations" section. Here, I share my thoughts based on the results I had from the many trials of making macarons with basic meringue. Additionally, all temperatures in the book are in Fahrenheit unless otherwise noted.

The best pastry chefs understand the structure and function of each ingredient, its interaction with other ingredients, and its reaction to the surroundings, including the temperature in the oven. This enables the chef to make adjustments to the given variables, regardless of a specific recipe. I'm not a pastry chef, just a pastry-chef-at-heart. However, I am a scientist and have always valued the details of the scientific method: Ask a question, do your research, and write down what you think will happen—this is your hypothesis. Perform an experiment to test your hypothesis, analyze your results, draw a conclusion, and write down your results. The beauty of this method is that you can go back to the beginning and make a change to the process in order to get you closer to your desired results.

Macarons are like tiny, blank canvases. You can color them in a multitude of colors; you can sprinkle on décor such as edible glitter; you can paint them with melted, colored white chocolate or white Crisco; you can use other types of ground nuts. And you can also play with a variety of fillings—a red-colored macaron might be flavored with a raspberry-chocolate ganache, a raspberry jam, raspberry buttercream, or lemon curd.

The discs may be made a week in advance and stored in air-tight freezer bags, within a covered container, at room temperature; place the container in the freezer for longer storage. Most fillings can be mixed ahead of time as well and kept in the fridge. Assembled sandwiches must be matured in the fridge for 12 to 48 hours prior to serving. Macarons are time-savers and have many possibilities.

I suggest that you read through the entire book then venture forward and bake a batch. Follow my recipe for almond macaron discs exactly as I have written it. The recipe is at the end of the book and is written step-by-step. It's practically foolproof; don't change the ingredients or the process until you have followed the recipe at least once. Don't let all the scientific stuff in the book scare you into not even trying. Jump in and make some!

I also made a corresponding video for my perfect macaron recipe. Visit YouTube.com and enter the keywords "macarons math, science, and art."

The Math Equation

Perfect macarons = even and quick heating + rough then tender macaronage + very stable meringue,

or

$$Y = a + b + c,$$

where Y has distinguishable feet and a solid base, is about ¼ inch thick, is smooth on the top, and has minimal empty spaces.

A change in any of the variables—the oven's heat, macaronage, meringue stability—could leave you with a tray of ugly-duckling macarons. Worse, you could end up with beautiful, but hollow cookies—nice feet, smooth top, and omg, as empty as unfilled plastic Easter eggs.

I have intentionally arranged these variables in this specific order because your oven plays the biggest role in the equation. If you bake in an electric oven instead of a convection oven, you must modify your macaronage technique and your ingredients. I will use this order for the duration of the book to explain to you the science behind these awesome cookies.

Hands-Down-You-Gottas

Macarons are really not as difficult to make as you might think. If you do a few things at the very beginning, you will definitely end up with pretty and delicious cookies. Hollow macs or cookies with air pockets may take a bit of troubleshooting, but they are still beautiful and yummy after they have been filled and matured in the fridge.

There are some fundamentals that a beginner should do. The following hands-down-you-gottas can only help you make perfect macs: (1) use an oven thermometer inside your oven; (2) weigh your ingredients; (3) cook on a low humidity day or keep your doors closed with the heater or air conditioner turned on; (4) age your eggs uncovered for at least three days at about 72 degrees Fahrenheit; (5) sift your almond flour through a fine-mesh sieve, whether you buy it or grind it yourself, if it looks moist, dry it; (6) leave some meringue inflated to give your batter more structure and stability; (7) test a small spoonful of batter in a small bowl before filling your piping bag; (8) depending on the volume or number of servings, you may need up to six, professional-grade, half-sheet pans; (9) bake for an extra minute or two if you are not sure the macarons are cooked; (10) bake one tray on the top, middle, and bottom of your oven to see which produces the best results; (11) keep a baking stone in the oven while the oven preheats.

A QUICKY-LIST OF THINGS YOU WILL NEED

Just in case you want to know what you will need to make macarons before reading through the book—in addition to your typical kitchen occupants—here you go:

Tools

Oven thermometer, kitchen scale, coffee grinder, fine-mesh strainer, half-sheet pans, silicone mats, parchment paper, cooling racks, cake decorating or piping bags, round cake decorating tips and couplers, plastic wrap, electric stand mixer, rubber spatula, clean kitchen towels, non-stick spray, food processor, baking stone, freezer-gallon bags, toothpicks, containers with covers

Ingredients

Six large egg whites, caster sugar, tapioca starch, cream of tartar, almond flour, powdered sugar, powdered or gel food coloring

MATTER AND MOLECULES

This is a very simplistic description of matter and molecules. Matter is made up of atoms and exists as solids, liquids, and gases; atoms have smaller parts called electrons, protons, and neutrons. Heat causes matter to change from one form to another, such as the water in egg whites turning into steam while the macaron batter bakes.

Matter is created when molecules or compounds bind together, such as hydrogen and oxygen binding together to form water. For simplicity, I will use the term "molecule" to refer to proteins, carbohydrates, fats, water, and even salt. When bonds are broken and made—like the protein bonds in egg whites—you end up with matter in a different form. In the case of meringue, you may start with slimy egg whites and rough sugar, but you end up with soft, fluffy meringue.

Molecules interact with the environment. The temperature, humidity, baking surfaces, and the number of molecules of a particular substance—such as the ratio of granulated sugar to egg whites—play a role in making macarons. The type of bowl you use, whether or not there is fat on your tools, and the speed at which you set your beaters all have some impact on the molecules in your recipe, thus determining the success or failure of making macaron discs.

ACIDS AND BASES

An acid is defined as a molecule that gives away a positively charged proton while a base accepts the positively charged proton. Acids taste sour; bases taste bitter and are slippery.

Acids and bases play a role in making perfect macaron cookies. The acidity or alkalinity of the ingredients in the macaron batter affects the batter's rise, its spread, and its texture. Acids and bases interact with each other, producing the gas that helps batters rise and spread as they bake.

OVENS AND BAKING HEAT

Once in the oven, the rate of the reaction of the molecules from the materials in your oven—walls of the oven, oven rack, baking pans, parchment paper, silicon mats, macaron batter—does affect the final look and texture of your macaron discs. If your oven does not apply a sufficient amount of heat quickly, you will have to modify your macaron recipe so that the batter bakes correctly in your specific oven.

Gas and Electric Ovens

Gas and electric home ovens emanate heat via heating elements located on the top or bottom of the oven; some ovens have both elements. The heat from these types of ovens travels to your pans and thus your baked goods as radiant and conductive heat. Paula Figoni, in her book, How Baking Works, does an excellent job explaining the difference between the two types of heat, "… imagine two teams of ten people, each arranged in a row. Each team must pass a ball from the first person to the last. The first team does this quickly by having the first person in the row toss the ball to the last person. The second team passes the ball by handing it from one person to the next, until the ball finally reaches the last person. Think of the first team as radiation and the second team as conduction." Heat is transferred from the oven to the macarons via the molecules in the air, the metal in the oven, the parchment paper or silicone mat, and the batter; radiant and conduction heat cook the macarons simultaneously.

The temperature in the front, back, middle, top, and bottom parts of the same oven may be different. Opening the oven door causes your oven temperature to drop; this may stimulate the oven to pile on the heat quickly until it reaches the desired temperature, temporarily becoming very hot. Ultimately, the temperature may become chaotic in there, swinging by as much as 20 degrees Fahrenheit.

Convection Ovens

Convection ovens use a fan to circulate hot air around your baked goods. This dries and cooks—or permanently sets—the structure of whatever it is you are baking. Convection ovens are the best ovens to bake macarons in because they quickly dry and set the raw meringue, thus leaving you with full macarons as opposed to hollow macarons; convection ovens are not great for your typical cakes and cookies. Some gas and electric ovens come with a convection feature. That is, you can press a button to turn the fan on or off. The fans in a convection oven can lead to a few weird-looking macaron discs. Consider placing the sheet of batter out-of-the-way of the fan if your macs are coming out lopsided and cracked.

Baking Considerations for Your Oven

Professional kitchens primarily use convection ovens that can hold several baking pans at one time—they bake massive amounts of batter in as little time as possible. This means that the last pan of batter doesn't sit out for two to three hours from the time the batter was piped—something that happens in most home kitchens. Batter that must be baked in multiple rounds sit out too long and the wait could cause the meringue to collapse. This increases the likelihood your cookies will be hollow.

If you don't have a convection oven, you must take steps to maintain a steady oven temperature as much as you can, getting the heat to your macs quickly while minimizing excessive browning. You must also take measures to reduce the amount of moisture in your batter.

Thermometers

An oven thermometer will help you gauge the actual heat produced in your oven. You will be able to see if your oven fluctuates a lot or a little, and take steps to make any necessary changes, such as using a baking stone.

Baking Stone

Shirley Corriher, in her book, BakeWise, advises bakers that she preheats a ¾-inch thick baking stone on the rack that is at the lower third of her oven. She then places her baking pans directly on the stone. The preheated stone enhances the volume of baked goods before the tops brown and the bottoms burn.

While you don't want too much rise from the macaron discs, a baking stone can potentially maintain a more even oven temperature. First, place the stone in the middle of the oven then place your tray of macs directly on the stone. If the heat is insufficient, move both to the lower rack.

Foil Shield

Macarons that are too close to an upper heating element or are baked at high temperatures may brown quickly. Position one of your oven racks immediately below the upper element of your oven. Tear a sheet of heavy duty foil and fold it so it is slightly larger than your baking pan. Place it on the rack to shield the heat from your cookies as they bake.

On the other hand, you may need the heat from the upper element to set, or cook, the surface of the discs. Bake a few pans with the foil shield and the remaining pans without the foil shield; take note of which works better for your oven.

Baking Pans

The composition of the baking pans you use does affect your macarons. Light-colored pans do not absorb as much heat as dark pans, while heavy-duty pans made of aluminum distribute heat very well. Changes in the terrain of your baking pans may cause your macaron discs to bake unevenly.

Consider purchasing heavy-duty, dark-colored half-sheet pans if you are having problems with the heat in your oven. The dark pans will get heat to your macarons faster than the shiny pans. Heavy-duty pans will distribute that heat evenly and are less likely to warp. Lopsided pans will cause your macs to bake into less-than-perfect circles.

You may need an extra baking pan to serve as a nesting pan for your tray of macs. Nesting simply means that the pans can snugly fit inside each other and stack one on top of the other. By using this extra barrier, you can place your macs as far away as possible from the upper element in your oven without the bottoms of the macs becoming too brown.

Silicone Mats

Silicone mats are thick compared to parchment paper. The mats increase the distance the heat must travel between the hot pan and the macaron batter, thus having an effect on your baked macarons. It takes the heat longer to get the gases going therefore macarons baked on a silicone mat will generally have shorter feet than macarons baked on parchment paper.

I prefer the silicone mats because they do not ripple compared to parchment sheets … and I don't have to wash the pan after every batch!

Parchment Paper

Manufacturers use different ingredients and different proportions of materials when making parchment paper. Keep in mind that if you change your brand of parchment paper, it could change the final look of your macaron discs. The molecules in the new paper may react differently with the molecules in the batter you have been using forever. Test a few circles of macaron batter on a new sheet of parchment so you don't waste a whole batch. Keep your normal baking mat or sheet on hand just in case. Because heat travels to the macaron batter faster when using parchment paper compared to using silicone mats, you will have to bake these trays at a slightly lower temperature than the temperature used with silicone mat-lined trays.

Results and Recommendations

Filling five to six trays with piped batter enabled me to test multiple levels of my oven, to bake with double pans, and to use or leave out the foil shield. I found that in my oven, it's best to bake at the lowest rack with a preheated baking stone and to stack one tray of macs on top of an empty tray.

Get to know your oven. If your oven has an upper and a lower element, it may be best to bake on the lowest rack, minimizing excessive browning from the top. To prevent the bottom from browning, nest the pan of piped batter into another pan that is exactly the same. Anytime you change the level or rack at which you are baking your macs, move the oven thermometer as well. Make a note that when you set the oven dial to 310 degrees Fahrenheit, for example, the thermometer inside is actually reading at 320 or 345 degrees Fahrenheit. This could happen because your oven needs to be calibrated. Also observe and notate how the temperature varies within the specified time that you are baking a tray. Because ovens work the way they do, the temperature fluctuations will eventually settle down to a specific temperature on the thermometer inside the oven.

TECHNIQUES

Whipping the Meringue

Stirring, beating, and whipping egg whites are multiple techniques used to unfold the proteins in egg whites. Under whipping egg whites does not enable the protein structure to form a very strong network. Whipping too fast causes the proteins to form big, unstable air bubbles. Slow, moderate whipping builds small air bubbles that are very stable.

Results and Recommendations

Whipping the egg whites at high speeds for more than a minute yielded too many air bubbles—and big bubbles at that. I found moderate whipping one of the keys to making perfect macarons. If you don't have a Kitchen Aid, use whatever it is you have, but follow the speed pattern indicated below.

Whip the egg whites at a medium speed for most of the whipping duration. Start at number 4 on the Kitchen Aid stand mixer, 4.5 quart model. Mix for six minutes to dissolve the sugar, cream of tartar, and starch. Increase the speed to medium-high, 5 on the Kitchen Aid, for nine minutes. Stop the mixer then add the coloring. Whip on high, or the number 6 on the Kitchen Aid, for 1 minute. If your meringue has not reached a stiff peak, continue whipping at level 6 for 30 seconds. Check the meringue again; the meringue should form a small ball inside the whisk and make stiff, though not super stiff peaks.

Macaronage of the Mixtures

This is a process of combining the nut mixture with the meringue. Some recipes require gentle folding while others utilize vigorous mixing. The end result of the macaronage technique is to deflate most of the air bubbles so that you end up with a flowing batter instead of stiff dough. The batter must be thin enough so that when you pipe a circle of batter, the point that remains "melts" into the surrounding batter. The batter must also be firm enough to maintain a round, cohesive form. If you over-deflate your batter, the surfaces of your baked macs will collapse, and the feet could ooze out around the perimeter. You will see dimples, and the discs will appear to have wet or blotchy spots. In essence, you have destroyed too much of the protein network for the macs to maintain their structure.

Results and Recommendations

I tried combining the mixture gently at first so as not to get powder everywhere; this was followed by thoroughly deflating the bubbles via smearing the mixture against the sides of the bowl. After several trials, I decided this intense macaronage was not a good technique. I started following Chef Martin Brunner's method of complete incorporation of a portion of the meringue, followed by gentle folding of the remaining meringue. I also discovered that sometimes I didn't have enough meringue to form a flowing batter. Thus, I began to take out a little bit of the almond flour and powdered sugar mixture prior to starting the macaronage.

Reserve a ½ cup of the almond flour and powdered sugar mixture. Do this by taking an adult dinner spoon and pouring the mixture over the ½-cup measuring cup. Use a straight edge knife to flatten the surface of the mixture in the cup. Set aside.

Note: I have never needed to use all of the dry ingredients in my recipe. Once I am done piping the batter, I pour this dry mix into a separate container. When I have 13 ounces of proportionately correct flour and sugar, I will try using it in this same recipe—in lieu of measuring out the almond flour and powdered sugar again. I'll post updates on this particular trial to my website.

Scoop half of the meringue out of the whipping bowl and thoroughly incorporate it into the dry mixture; do this by folding the batter onto itself and pressing the batter against the sides and bottom of the bowl. It's not a matter of being gentle or rough, just being thorough. Once the mixtures are well mixed, lift some batter up with the spatula then let it fall back into the bowl. Look at your batter closely; it will look pretty thick. Add a small portion of the remaining meringue. Incorporate well again. Look at your batter; it should look thinner, with the ribbons slowly blending into the surrounding batter. Add the last of the meringue and tenderly fold it in—now is the time to be gentle. Incorporate thoroughly.

Test the batter as described below.

Test Your Batter

Scoop a small amount of batter out of the bowl with a small cereal spoon. Ladle the batter into a mound in a plastic bowl, trailing the batter on the top to mimic the point of a piped macaron. Tap the plate on the counter. If the tip disappears, your batter is ready. If not, return the batter to the bowl and fold 10 more strokes. Test again.

Piping

Filling the Pastry Bag

A long time ago I was wrapping the dough for guyuria, a Guam cookie. I realized that if I could wrap the cookie dough, I could wrap cake frosting too. I now use plastic wrap for everything that I have to put into a piping bag, including macaron batter. Basically, you want to wrap the batter as you would an oval-shaped hard candy. Lay a 16-inch sheet of plastic wrap on the counter. Mound about 1 cup of batter in the center of the plastic wrap, at a diagonal. The ends of the batter should be pointing to opposite corners of the diagonal. Fold the lower half of the plastic wrap over the mound of batter, pressing it against the batter to eliminate air bubbles. Roll the batter all the way up toward the other end of the plastic wrap. Twist the ends and tuck under the mound; repeat with remaining batter. To use, grab one mound of batter. Untuck one end and clip the excess plastic wrap. Squeeze a bit of batter up toward the opening and insert this end into the prepared piping bag.

Figure 2 - Wrapping batter or filling in plastic wrap before piping

Drawing the Patterns

Drawing a pattern on the back of parchment paper can help you pipe even circles until you get the hang of piping without a pattern. I found the easiest thing to do is to use Microsoft Word or a similar program.

Figure 3 - Making the pattern for parchment paper

Open a blank document then insert a circle. You'll have to adjust the size, print the document, and then readjust the size of the circle back on your computer until you get a circle that measures about 1 1/16 to 1 1/8 of an inch in diameter. A diameter is the distance across opposite sides of a circle, running through the middle.

Copy and paste the circle so you end up with three circles in a horizontal line, as straight as possible; space them evenly. Select two circles then copy and paste them below the first row. Stagger the row of two circles such that the circles are between the three circles above.

Copy and paste the rows so you end up with five, alternating, staggered rows of circles. Print one sheet.

Lay the sheet on the baking pan then put a piece of parchment over them, wrong side up. Align the left sides of the pattern and the parchment together if you are a right-handed person; align the right sides if you are a lefty. Instead of tracing each circle in its entirety, mark only the top, bottom, and side borders of each circle with a dash. When you pipe the batter with your bag perpendicular to the parchment, the batter will spread in a circle; stop when you hit the marked borders.

Begin your tracings from left to right if you are a righty so you don't smear pencil markings all over the place; work right to left if you are a lefty.

Spray the pan with non-stick spray.

Turn the parchment right side up. Carefully apply the parchment paper to the prepared pan as if applying tint to a window or wallpaper to a wall.

Piping the Circles

Start in the middle of each pattern, squeezing the piping bag gently and keeping the bag perpendicular to the baking sheet. If you keep the tip about one-eighth of an inch from the pan, you will automatically pop some of the bigger air bubbles as you squeeze the batter out. Lift the bag quickly then move to the next pattern.

Tapping

Once the macaron batter has been piped onto the baking sheets, the entire sheet must be tapped on the counter. Just like dropping a batter-filled cake pan, this process helps bring air bubbles to the surface. Unpopped air bubbles can form pockets in the finished product or can cause the surface of the macarons to crack as they bake.

Results and Recommendations

I experimented with a little tapping, a lot of tapping, gently tapping, and vigorous tapping. The middle-of-the-road works best here with 8 to 10 repetitions.

Hold the short ends of the pan in each hand then gently hit the tray against a non-breakable surface about eight times. Starting on one side of the tray, go across the tray and pop any visible bubbles. Go back to the beginning and pop again because more bubbles will rise; it should take you no more than 1 minute to pop bubbles. Set aside to dry.

Drying

Drying the piped batter enables the batter to form a crust and become hard so that the batter is strong enough to resist cracking as it bakes. In a very dry kitchen, this may take only 30 minutes. Touch a few buttons of batter after 30 minutes. If they are dry and do not make an indentation, the batter is ready. If they are still wet or if they make an indentation, let them continue drying.

There are gases in the air that you whip into the meringue. Likewise, water transforms into steam while the macaron batter bakes. This creates the rise in the macaron discs. Due to the crust on the surface of the batter, the gases cannot escape from the top of the macarons like other baked goods. The gases must escape, and they do so at the base of the cookies, thus creating the feet. If your batter does not harden on the outside, the gases escape from the top, leaving your macs feetless and cracked.

Results and Recommendations

By the time I finished piping the last tray of macs, the buttons of batter on the first tray had dried; however, I could still make an indentation on them. It took about 45 minutes of drying in my kitchen before the first tray was dry and hard—no indentations. I always make a note of the current time when I am done piping each tray. This way, I'm not left guessing how long each tray has been sitting out. It takes me about 3 to 5 minutes to pipe one tray of batter AND pop the bubbles.

If your first tray is not dry by the time you are done piping, consider cracking your oven door open as it preheats. Set the oven to 250 degrees Fahrenheit and place all your trays on adjacent counters.

If your piped batter takes more than an hour to dry and you are unable to bake all your trays at once, chances are the meringue will become unstable and will collapse after they bake. Go ahead and bake all the trays anyway and take notes so you can use the data at for your next batch.

Test for Doneness and Baking Time

Is it done? Is it done? Depending on a particular recipe, the macs may still stick to the parchment or silicone mat whether or not they are done.

In my experience, if the macs are not cooked through, they will deflate and soften too much when filled; they are also less likely to remain chewy if the insides are not done.

Ms. Humble, of notsohumblepie.blogspot.com, says that it's best to err on baking the macs a little too long so they are hard and dry. Once you fill the macs and let them rest in the fridge for a day, they'll soften up.

Results and Recommendations

Baking the macs was the most brutal variable of all my trials! It all came down to how much moisture was in the batter from the egg whites and the flour, and how stable the meringue was.

Press the tops of one or two macs when the baking time is up; if they don't squish down, make much of an indentation, or otherwise move, they are done. If they are not done, continue to bake the macs, checking every minute. Do not increase the baking temperature or the macarons will become too brown. If you are using a foil shield, remove it.

Partial-Batch Baking

Each new macaron batter recipe you try can behave differently in your oven. If you are making macs for the first time or if this is your first attempt of a particular recipe, you will save yourself heartache by baking a few macs at a time on separate trays. Having six trays gives you many opportunities to experiment with different rack levels, temperatures, and baking durations, using the same batter.

Results and Recommendations

I found that it was advantageous to have six baking pans, five silicone mats, and parchment paper. I could test multiple baking and oven variables with one batter.

Pipe six buttons of batter in the middle of a baking sheet. Bake according to the directions of the recipe. Bake on the middle rack of your oven if this is your first time making macarons; bake at the rack level you normally use if you've made macs before. Depending on your results, you may have to change the level at which you bake the macs, the oven temperature, or the baking duration. By baking in small batches initially, you have enough batter and pans to test a new macaron recipe in your oven.

TOOLS

Kitchen Scales

It is vital that you use a kitchen scale to measure an accurate amount of each of your ingredients. If the ratios are off, the end product has a higher probability of being a flop. A scale that measures weight using increments of one-tenth of an ounce is more readable—more precise—than a scale that measures weight using increments of two grams.

Whether you use an electronic or mechanical scale, the scale should be calibrated against a known weight. This ensures it is accurately measuring your ingredients.

Most macaron recipes give weight in grams. Grams can be easily converted by searching the Internet. Enter the key words "convert weight in grams to weight in ounces", and your search engine will find you a conversion calculator. All solids and liquids should be measured in weight. That is, 5 ounces of egg whites is 5 ounces on a weight scale, NOT 5 ounces in a volume-measuring pitcher.

Strainers

You need a fine-mesh strainer to sift ground almonds into a fine powder. The hole of the wire mesh should be less than 1/16 of an inch; the needle of a small thumbtack should not be able to go through the hole. Don't use your old, somewhat misshapen strainers. Get a new one and save it just for the ground nuts. Also, check your nut strainer throughout the years as you will eventually need to replace it.

Fat-Free Tools

Egg yolks, butter, shortening, and oil are types of fats. Fat molecules cover protein molecules, decreasing the ability of the protein molecules to unfold and bind back together. Furthermore, fat molecules take up space on the surface of air bubbles, decreasing the strength of any molecule network that does form. Egg whites contaminated with fat molecules are highly prone to deflating or may not whip up well at all.

Boil water in a microwaveable pitcher then pour the water over the beater, whipping bowl, and rubber spatula. Dry all of your tools completely with a fat-free kitchen towel, standing at room temp for a few minutes before using.

Beaters and Whisks

Ever whip egg whites using an old whisk with its tines off-center? How does it compare to a new whisk with lots of tines? The more tines your beater or whisk has, the better and more quickly it will incorporate air into your meringue. Additionally, beaters and whisks with thick tines produce large, unstable air bubbles; beaters and whisks with thin tines create smaller, more stable air bubbles. Of course, if you use a stand-mixer compared to a hand-held beater, it will do the job that much more effectively.

Bowls

Stainless steel, glass, and copper bowls do not absorb fat and odors like plastic, so they are better to use when making macaron discs. Save the plastic for sugar cookies.

The copper in copper bowls reacts with a specific protein in egg whites. This copper-coated protein hardens at a higher temperature in the oven. The finished meringue from a copper bowl will have somewhat of a golden color. Copper mixing bowls are readily and inexpensively available at online stores. Copper bowls for the Kitchen Aid mixers are several hundred dollars.

Ms. Humble attests that a copper bowl helps her make the best macarons. Meanwhile, in BakeWise, Shirley Corriher notes that if you want to achieve volume in your finished baked product—like soufflés—use a copper mixing bowl. However, she warns, leave the cream of tartar out of the recipe or it will add an excessive amount of copper into your baked goods.

Many have produced wonderful macaron discs without a copper bowl, but if you have a couple of hundred dollars to spare and are really having a difficult time with macarons, go ahead and get a copper bowl.

Piping Bag

There are a variety of brands of piping or cake decorating bags. Use what you are comfortable with as long as they are squeaky clean and dry. I grew up with Wilton-brand products. I like the 12-inch disposable cake decorating bags because they fit perfectly in my hand; the 16-inch and bigger bags are much too big for me to efficiently pipe nice circles. I also use Wilton couplers and the #12 rounded tips to pipe my macaron batter. Couplers are the two-piece plastic parts that hold a decorating tip in place when using a piping bag.

Figure 4 - An assembled piping bag

MAIN INGREDIENTS

Egg Whites

Structure

Egg whites contain water and protein. The special blend of proteins in the whites provides the framework needed to hold trapped air when the whites are whipped. Egg whites are alkaline in nature.

An egg white is almost 90% water. The longer the time between when an egg is laid and when an egg is used, the greater the loss of moisture, even in the shell. Still, the egg white is water-rich. The sell-by date on the egg carton is the 30-day mark for USDA-graded eggs. By the time you get the eggs home, they are already a few weeks old. The older an egg is, the more the egg white breaks down and becomes watery. Watery eggs don't whip up very well. It takes about six weeks for an egg white in the shell to become too watery for whipping purposes.

Fresh eggs are best when you want a very stable meringue. However, they have too much moisture compared to older eggs that have been in your fridge for a while. If you use fresh egg whites in your meringue, it will take too long for the piped macaron batter to dry. By the time the batter dries, the meringue will be very unstable and collapse as it bakes.

The temperature, humidity, and air currents inside your house affect the amount of moisture that is lost when you age your eggs at room temperature.

Function

Beating egg whites simultaneously unfolds the proteins and incorporates air bubbles. When this happens, the unfolded proteins move to the surface of the air bubbles and attach to other protein molecules. A network of air bubbles and strong protein bonds is formed, thus the transformation of clear liquid egg whites to white, "solid" egg whites. The proper unfolding and rebonding of egg whites work best when the whites are at room temperature, about 70 degrees Fahrenheit.

Common Practices

In the macaron world, some people swear by "aged" egg whites, while others say it's not necessary. To "age" an egg white, the egg is cracked and the two parts are separated. The white is kept in the fridge for three to five days then left to sit at room temperature several hours before use. Egg whites are also left uncovered at room temperature to age. The intent of "aging" an egg white is to remove moisture.

In Theory

Farm-fresh eggs would be best for macarons because they make more stable meringues. Old eggs, the eggs that have been in your fridge for a few weeks, are better because they do not have as much moisture compared to farm-fresh eggs. Aging farm-fresh eggs at room temperature for two days would be the happy marriage of the two.

Results and Recommendations

Eggs, oh my gosh! I go through 4 dozen during an average week in my household. However, I practically doubled that as I worked through trial after trial of making macarons.

I found that eggs are best when they are aged uncovered at room temperature, compared to being aged uncovered in the fridge. Within two days, 5.5 ounces of eggs, aged in my dining room, lost 1 ounce compared to 0.3 ounces in the fridge. I also discovered that the temperature of my whites was slightly less than the temp on my thermostat. I used the whites as is because they were only about 67 degrees Fahrenheit.

Some folks "age" their eggs in the microwave. I gave it a shot during one of my mad-scientist moments. I just finished trial 14 and all the cookies were hollow. I figured it was a perfect time to try the microwave out. I weighed 4.8 ounces of room temperature, old egg whites then heated them in the microwave on high. I started with 8 seconds, added 8 more seconds followed by two, 5-second intervals. I placed the bowl on the scale, and I was amazed that the whites were losing weight. I figured the water was evaporating as I could see the weight drop by 0.1 ounces. By the time I was ready to mix the almond flour and powdered sugar, the weight dropped to 3.8 ounces. I thought I'd have a good batch! Not. I reweighed the eggs and the weight was back up to 4.7 ounces. Ugh! Oh well, it was a good experiment. At the end of trial 15, I had full macs, but their surfaces were still blotchy, collapsing in the middle. To emphasize the point, eggs must be aged for at least 72 hours at room temperature for best results.

The weight of egg whites decrease as they lose water. If you measure 4 ounces of egg whites then age them, you will end up with less egg whites to make your meringue. The best thing to do is measure an extra ounce or two of egg whites before you age them. Make a note of their total weight. Just prior to making your meringue, weigh the egg whites again and make a note of the new weight. Finally, measure out the exact amount of egg whites you need for your recipe. You can figure out the rate of moisture loss according to the equation below:

Starting weight of newly separated egg whites – weight of the same egg whites after three days ÷ three days.

Or, for the egg whites from five large eggs,

(6.3 oz. – 5.1 oz.) / 3 days = 1.2 oz / 3 days

= 1.2/3

= 0.4 oz. lost per day over three days for 6.3 ounces of newly separated egg whites aged at about 71 to 73 degrees Fahrenheit. If you do not lose at least 1.2 ounces per day from about 6.3 total ounces of egg whites, you must age the eggs another day or two.

Before whipping your whites, check their temperature. Place the probe of a digital cooking thermometer into the bowl of whites without touching the bowl. The temperature displayed will probably not be the same as the thermostat of your house that reads 70 degrees Fahrenheit. If it's more than 5 degrees cooler, warm the egg whites to room temperature. Use a double broiler to heat your egg whites to about 70 degrees then whip them. A double boiler is simply a clean, stainless steel bowl atop a smaller pot of simmering water; the bowl should not touch the water. The egg whites go in the stainless steel bowl.

I also aged four egg whites—or 4.8 ounces of whites—for two days. My rate of moisture loss was 0.5 ounces per day. I'm sure the initial volume of whites had a slight effect on the amount of loss. However, what I noticed more was that the egg whites that were aged for three days were much thicker than the egg whites aged for two days. For trial 18, the macs were definitely more perfect using three-day old eggs as opposed to trial 17's two-day old eggs.

Egg White Powder

Structure

Egg white powder is the dehydrated version of liquid egg whites. Liquid egg whites are dried until there is less than 5 percent of water left in the whites. It is also treated with an enzyme to remove the small amount of glucose found in liquid whites. Dried egg whites are kept in a hot room for pasteurization. This heat treatment enhances the strength and whipping ability of the proteins.

Function

Dried egg whites, or egg white powder, gives a better feel to meringues and enhances the meringue's stability. It gives royal icing, the icing that hardens, a shiny coat.

Common Practice

A few recipes do include egg white powder.

In Theory

Egg white powder increases the protein content of the meringue without the added moisture. This would be one way of enhancing meringue stability.

Results and Recommendations

I have yet to use egg white powder. After reviewing the science of meringue and the individual ingredients, I opted out of using egg white powder. Instead, I focused on adding a starch and changing the whipping speed of the egg whites.

Meringue Powder

Structure

Meringue powder is a mixture of primarily pasteurized, dried egg whites, and sugar, starch, gums, cream of tartar, and flavorings.

Function

It helps stabilize meringues, especially when it is humid.

Common Practice

Most recipes use dried egg white powder instead of meringue powder. I took a macaron class with Chef Martin, who used meringue powder for his Italian meringue; he did not use it for the basic meringue.

In Theory

While egg white powder and meringue powder are different, meringue powder serves the same function by combining egg white powder with other stabilizers. Thus, it should enhance stability similarly to, if not better than, just egg white powder.

Results and Recommendations

I used meringue powder once or twice then nixed that ingredient. I started to focus more on adding starch, whipping the whites, macaronage, and the eggs themselves.

Sugar

Structure

The sugar most of us are familiar baking with is sucrose. Other types of sugar include lactose, fructose, maltose, and glucose. Sucrose comes in dry crystal form, such as granulated and powdered sugars or syrups like honey and molasses. Sugars love water and therefore pull water from its surroundings, including from your batter and from the air.

Highly refined sugar like granulated table sugar, super-fine or extra-fine granulated sugar, and caster sugar have practically no impurities. Any impurities in the sugar you use can cause the sugar to recrystalize after it has dissolved. The smaller the sugar crystal, the better it dissolves. There is a noticeable difference between the crystal sizes of granulated sugar, superfine sugar, and caster sugar.

Most powdered sugar brands contain a tiny bit of cornstarch. The added starch helps to stabilize and stiffen meringues. Powdered sugar is sold—albeit difficult to find—without cornstarch. Some swear by the use of one or the other for macarons.

Function

Sugar has many roles, including acting as a tenderizer, adding sweetness, enhancing the browning of baked goods, retaining moisture, and extending shelf life. Sugar slows whipping and reduces the volume of the meringue, which is generally why sugar is added after a mixture is foamy or at the soft peak stage. Shirley Corriher advises that it is best to add sugar too early instead of too late; if you wait too long to add the sugar, the meringue will dry out.

In the case of meringues, sugar stabilizes the egg whites by absorbing the water from the protein molecules. The less water in the protein molecules, the faster your meringue will set and harden. Sugar gives meringue a satiny sheen and creates a thick liquid film that helps prevent air bubbles from collapsing.

The ratio of sugar to egg whites in a French meringue should be equal. That is, the weight of sugar should equal the weight of egg whites. Note that Italian meringues for macarons have double to triple the weight of sugar to that of egg whites. The higher sugar ratio and the fact that the sugar is cooked into syrup is why Italian meringues are supposedly more stable than French meringues.

Common Practice

Most French meringue recipes require that granulated sugar be slowly added to egg whites at the soft peak stage. Pastry chef Stella of bravetart.com adds her sugar with the egg whites before she begins whipping; she uses a Kitchen Aid stand mixer and whips for 9 to 10 minutes at medium to high speeds.

In Theory

The size of the sugar crystals makes a difference in the outcome of some baked goods. Consider the large sugar crystals that top muffins and the smaller sugar crystals of granulated sugar used to make the muffin batter. There is a reason why uncooked frostings use powdered sugar and cooked frostings use granulated sugar. If you have access to caster sugar, and the bag is explicitly labeled as "caster" or "castor" sugar, then the sugar crystals will easily dissolve in the whites. Caster sugar can be combined with the egg whites at the very beginning while unpulvarized granulated sugar should be added slowly to the barely-soft-peaked whites.

Results and Recommendations

I've only used caster sugar during my trials simply because it is more convenient. Caster sugar is very expensive compared to table sugar. On the other hand, my recipe only calls for a small amount, so if you buy a small bag of caster sugar, it will last you many, many batches.

Some folks suggest pulverizing table sugar in a blender until it is powdery. Once you have mastered my recipe then I think it should be fine to swap the sugars—if you pulverize the table sugar.

Nuts

Structure

Nuts contain mostly fat, but they also have fiber, protein, and water. Due to their fat content, nuts can spoil quickly; they become rancid and can develop an unpleasant odor.

Function

Nuts are used to enhance the flavor, texture, and visual appeal of foods. The volume of one nut in a recipe can generally be replaced with an equal volume of another nut, except for chestnuts; chestnuts have very little fat and plenty of water.

The greater the surface area of a nut that is exposed to the air, the greater the loss of moisture. The warmer the air temperature, the greater the loss of moisture as well. Nuts, including almonds, lose moisture when they are processed, such as taking raw almonds and roasting, slicing, slivering, blanching, or grinding them.

Common Practices

Many recipes call for store-bought almond flour, also called almond meal, because of its ultra fine texture. It definitely makes the whole macaron-making experience less taxing. Other recipes advise placing whole, blanched almonds and the powdered sugar in a food processor to produce a powder. Unblanched almonds are also used, but the flecks of skin are visible in the final cookies.

In Theory

Store-bought almond flour has been sitting on a shelf for some time, losing its natural moisture. Almond flour is freshest when you make your own at home, thus a stronger almond flavor and higher moisture content. Grinding nuts in a food processor does not yield a fine enough consistency for the ultra smooth surface of perfect macarons.

Figure 5 - The setup for grinding your own almond flour

Results and Recommendations

All the trials I did in which the macs were NOT hollow used store-bought flour. I could easily see the moisture and oil in the flour that I ground myself.

I would suggest using store-bought for your first time up to bat with this recipe. Once you know it works, grind your own nuts, but dry it in the oven or leave it uncovered at room temperature for a few days. Dry the flour in a 200-degree Fahrenheit oven for 30 minutes then cool the flour completely before using it.

I grind my nuts in a coffee grinder—reserved for nuts/spices only—then sift the resulting flour through a fine-meshed strainer. Once I mix the flour with the powdered sugar in the food processor, I sift it all again.

Cream of Tartar, Vinegar, Lemon Juice

Structure

Cream of tartar, vinegar, and lemon juice are all acids, and all are said to be acidic. Baking soda and Rolaids are bases, or are said to be basic. Milk is neutral; it is not acidic or basic. Though the chemical reaction of acid and base molecules is not so simple, it's about gaining and losing hydrogen particles.

Function

Acids in recipes have various roles, including helping to stabilize a meringue, lowering the temperature at which proteins bind back together, dissolving starch molecules, enhancing the effectiveness of baking soda, and minimizing the discoloration of fruits.

Common Practice

Some macaron recipes use cream of tartar. Cream of tartar helps increase the rebonding of the protein in egg whites. It helps stabilize the network of protein bonds during whipping, baking, folding, and piping. Too much cream of tartar leaves an off-taste.

In Theory

If you use "old" eggs, whip the whites properly and deflate the batter sufficiently, you should be okay without cream of tartar. It would not hurt your meringue to use cream of tartar.

Results and Recommendations

Without a convection oven, I have opted to use cream of tartar. I need all the help I can get to avoid hollow macs. I've never used vinegar or lemon juice.

If the recipe you are using calls for cream of tartar, go ahead and use it. Again, consider the individual ingredients and the in-the-moment environmental conditions to help you decide whether you should add or subtract cream of tartar. On my part, I'd rather not take a chance and end up with hollow macarons.

Cocoa Powder

Structure

Growing on cacao trees are cacao pods, or cocoa pods. Inside each pod are 20 to 40 or so cocoa beans. The cocoa bean is like an almond. Crack the shell of the cocoa bean and inside is the cocoa nib. This nib is what is used to make cocoa and chocolate. The cocoa nib itself is made up of fat—cocoa butter—and other nonfat substances. These substances are collectively referred to as cocoa solids nonfat, and they include protein, carbohydrate, and acid molecules. The cocoa nibs are ground to a liquid-like consistency called chocolate liquor. Once cooled, the liquor hardens into a solid block and comes in several names, including unsweetened chocolate, bittersweet chocolate, and baking chocolate. To make cocoa powder, this solid block is heated and treated under high pressure. The fat drips out and the remaining "cake" is ground into natural cocoa powder. Cocoa powder is slightly acidic and contains starches, dextrins, and sugars.

Function

Cocoa powder adds flavor and color to baked goods. However, cocoa powder is also a drying agent; it pulls water away from the protein molecules in macaron batter.

Common Practice

Cocoa powder is whirled with the almond flour and powdered sugar in the food processor.

In Theory

Adding cocoa powder to a plain almond macaron recipe should help dry the cookies faster. The faster the protein molecules lose water, the faster the structure sets and the less likely your discs will be hollow.

Results and Recommendations

My second attempt at making macarons was a cocoa-flavored recipe. Looking back, some were hollow and some not. Thus, cocoa powder definitely aids in stabilizing the macs since the exact recipe without cocoa powder yielded hollow macs across all trays.

Consider adding 2 tablespoons of cocoa powder to a plain recipe that bakes beautifully but is hollow. Take notes.

Salt

Structure

Salt is made up of sodium and chloride.

Function

Salt is used in baked goods to enhance color and flavor. Salt is especially important in controlling yeast and enzyme activity in bread. It helps increase the strength of gluten. Salt makes meringue less stable. Meringues that use salt to balance the sugar may take a bit longer to whip up.

Common Practice

Many recipes include salt, perhaps because a pinch of salt is used in nearly every type of food cooked. Salt may also be used to balance the amount of sugar in a recipe.

In Theory

The addition of salt in your macaron recipes may lead to hollow and unstable macs.

Results and Recommendations

After the first few trials, I left the salt out. Because I was testing other more important variables, I cannot really say if salt helped or hurt my results.

When it comes to salt, if a recipe calls for it, go ahead and use it. Next time, consider leaving the salt out of the recipe; see if the cookies turn out better. Because salt makes the meringue less stable, it could be the reason your macs are hollow.

MACARON DISC FLAVORINGS

Extracts, Oils, and Liquors

Liquid flavorings add moisture to your macaron discs. It's best to save them for use in the fillings.

Infused Sugars, Herbs, Spices

Dry flavorings should enhance or compliment your filling. If you want vanilla macs, add spent vanilla beans to your caster sugar about one week before using the sugar. For herbs and spices, add ¼ to ½ teaspoon of the dried herb and 1/8 a teaspoon of the ground herb to the almond flour-powdered sugar mixture.

COLORING AGENTS

Liquids

Liquid colors add moisture to your batter. Don't waste your time and money chancing a flopped batch.

Powders and Gels

Powders do not add moisture to your batter compared to a tiny bit from gels. However, gel coloring is more widely available than powdered coloring. Colored powders may be purchased via online baking supply companies. Also, you may see flecks of primary-color powdered coloring inside the macaron discs if you use gel colors.

ENVIRONMENTAL CONCERNS

Humidity

Humidity is a measure of the amount of gaseous water—water in a gas state, commonly referred to as water vapor—in the atmosphere. High humidity means the air outside contains a lot of water; if you are outside and your skin feels sticky and wet, it is because the air is already full of water and your sweat cannot evaporate. Low humidity means the air outside contains very little water; if you are outside and your skin is dry, it is because the water on your skin is easily absorbed into the air around you.

Results and Recommendations

I have yet to use a humidity monitor in my kitchen, though I've been meaning to get one. I keep my house closed up and the heater turned on. I'll have to see how the macs turn out in the midst of North Carolina's very humid summers.

Consider turning your oven on to its lowest setting and cracking it open 10 minutes before you start making your meringue. Leave it on low until your piped buttons of batter are dry to the touch. Turn it to the necessary preheated temperature about 10 minutes prior to baking. This oven treatment will help keep your kitchen a bit on the drier side.

During highly humid conditions, this is a good time to do all you can to reduce moisture in your ingredients and enhance stability of your meringue—age your eggs for five days, dry your almond flour, use powdered food coloring, use vanilla sugar instead of vanilla extract, add cream of tartar, use a copper bowl, turn on the dehumidifier, close up the windows, and use your heater or air conditioner.

Temperature

Warm temperatures and air circulation increase the rate of moisture loss.

Results and Recommendations

It's wintertime here in North Carolina, so I have my heater turned on. I generally keep my thermostat between 70 and 73 degrees Fahrenheit.

Age your egg whites and dry your almond flour in warm and well-ventilated areas of your kitchen to ensure sufficient moisture is evaporated.

MACARON DIAMETER

Once you pipe the batter onto your mat or parchment paper, it will continue to spread. It will spread a bit more after you tap the pans.

I like the two-bite macaron: in two bites, you are done! I have not actually baked larger or smaller ones. If they are too small, they become difficult to fill without making a mess. I have seen pictures of large macarons; these are assembled with a piped filling and fruits.

The key in picking a size is to make it consistent per tray. Bear in mind that changing the size also changes the length of time the discs need to dry and bake.

MATURATION AND FILLINGS

Maturing macaron cookies means that you sandwich a filling using two macaron discs and store the filled cookies in the fridge. Most recommend a 24-hour maturation period. This enables the discs to absorb moisture from the filling, becoming soft and chewy instead of hard and crumbly. The maturation period also depends on the type of filling you use.

Soft Fillings

Macaron discs absorb moisture quickly from soft fillings compared to hard filings. Soft fillings include whipped cream, pastry cream, and cream cheese-based flavors. If you over-bake your macs or if they are really hard when they come out of the oven, it may take 24 hours to mature with a soft filling. Discs that are cooked but are not as hard may need as little as 12 hours using the same soft filling. Cookies with soft fillings that are matured too long become very mushy and lose their chewiness.

Firm Fillings

Stiff ganaches, very firm jams, nut pastes, and butter creams are delicious fillings and are excellent if you want to make your cookies 48 hours in advance. Ganache is basically a mixture of chocolate and heavy cream. A tad bit of butter and corn syrup may be added to enhance the ganache's color and texture. Nut pastes are usually softened with butter and simple syrup so the filling can be piped from a pastry bag.

Disc Thickness Matters

Thick macarons will take longer to soften compared to thin macarons. Keep this in mind as you chose your fillings. Soft fillings work well for thick cookies if the cookies have to mature in less than 24 hours; hard fillings are fine for thin cookies that you will need in the same amount of time. The thinner the cookies, the faster they mature, and the faster they become mushy.

Results and Recommendations

To me, the perfect macs are about ¼-inch thick because I can fill them with a sufficient amount of filling to derive the ultimate sensations—perfect crumb, perfect chew, perfect flavor!

Keep track of how your specific fillings change the texture of your cookies. By keeping track, you take out the guesswork for filling the same type of macarons later on.

STORING MACARONS

Unfilled

Unfilled macaron discs should be stored in air-tight containers, like freezer gallon bags. Stack only in a single layer per bag. Bags may be gently stacked in a large container with a cover. Keep the container at room temperature for up to two days. Place the sealed macs in your freezer if you will not be filling the discs thereafter. The macs do harden if left uncovered on your counter in a dry kitchen.

Filled

Filled macaron cookies should be placed in the fridge or in the freezer immediately. Refrigerated cookies will keep for two days in the fridge. Frozen macaron cookies store well in the freezer for one month and must be thawed in the fridge the night prior to serving.

QUICK REVIEW

This is just an at-a-glance summary of common problems and possible causes. The solutions will vary. Refer to the detailed explanations above and the scientific method below to figure out a solution specific to your recipe, tools, techniques, and environment.

Problem: Cracked Surface

Possible causes: large piece of nut, under deflated batter, insufficient drying time, heat too high

Problem: No Feet

Possible causes: insufficient heat, excess moisture in ingredients, under whipped meringue, insufficient drying time

Problem: Lopsided Cookies

Possible causes: under whipped meringue, warped paper or baking pan, uneven tapping, excess moisture in egg whites

Problem: Hollow Centers

Possible causes: unstable oven temperature, insufficient rest, unstable meringue

THE SCIENTIFIC METHOD FOR SOLVING MACARON PROBLEMS

This template for the scientific method is not necessary when you have a recipe that already works. However, this process will help you create new recipes or adjust an old recipe that starts to go crazy on you. Here's what I did for trial 17:

-Ask a Question

Would farm-fresh eggs that have been aged for two days produce perfect-top macs—no cave-ins—compared to the nearly perfect macs from old eggs that were also aged for two days?

-Research

After 15 attempts, I've learned plenty—starch is definitely needed; the moisture and stability of the meringue determines whether the macs cook quickly enough; unheated nesting pans prevent excessive browning from the bottom; the heat from the upper element is necessary to set the top of the macs so don't use a foil shield, at least in my oven.

-Make a Hypothesis

I believe that the farm-fresh eggs that were aged for two days should produce awesome-looking macs without any concavity because the farm-fresh eggs are supposed to give meringue more stability than the old eggs aged for just as long.

-Do the Experiment, that is, Make It Again

This experiment was trial 17.

-Analyze Data and Draw Conclusions

For the first two trays, the macs did not collapse in the oven. However, once I pulled the tray out and set on the stove top, the centers did begin to collapse. The collapsed area also looked moist. I cracked the door open for the last two trays.

-Report Your Results

The macs from the last two trays, in which I did crack open the oven door, were nearly perfect. The feet were ruffled, the tops were excellent, and they were not hollow. The only thing I did not like was that they were too browned at 315 degrees Fahrenheit. I ran out of trays to test at 310 degrees. My hypothesis proved to be wrong. Farm-fresh eggs aged for two days were not better than old eggs aged for two days.

-Sample Data Sheet

I found that keeping data on blank sheets of paper was very ineffective. Below is a picture of a spreadsheet I came up with to help clarify variables and observations. I did use the back of the sheet for extra notes.

Figure 6 - Sample data sheet for macaron experiments

GET CREATIVE

Once you have perfected your macaron discs using your oven, it's time to really have fun! It's best to test your décor on just a few macs before and after baking. There are many things you can use. For me, however, I try to maintain the experience of eating a soft, chewy cookie. Thus, I refrain from anything that is too crunchy or using a grainy décor in excess. The food coloring you used to color your batter is the primary décor. Sprinkles and paints should be used as accents, covering a very small area of the macarons. But this is your art, so create as you wish. It's always best to do a trial run before making these cookies for an event.

Sprinkles

There are so many to choose from—edible glitter, cocoa powder, cake sprinkles, sesame seeds, sugared flower petals, and more. The key here is to first see how the sprinkles will affect your macs as they bake. In my experience, macaron batter and Himalayan pink salt don't work well together while baking.

Paints

The paints to use include melted chocolate, melted white chocolate, melted white Crisco, and royal icing. Use a paint brush solely for edible paints. Melt your paint then brush a little bit on the top of your baked macs. Paints can also be used as the glue for sprinkles once the macs are baked, completely cooled, and at room temperature if they were stored in the freezer.

Fillings

Red macs are generally filled with a red jam; but a yellow mac would be a nice contrast to the red filling. Fill the cooled cookies with strawberry jam, blueberry jam, and maybe lemon curd. Distinguish the flavored filling with a brush of melted Crisco and red, blue, or yellow edible glitter.

Shapes

Macaron batter may be piped into various shapes, including hearts and letters of the alphabets. Be sure to keep the shapes and thickness as similar as possible so the macs bake evenly.

FROM MY LAB TO YOUR KITCHEN

To me, baking is so much more than eating sweet goodies. It's about making beautiful things that someone else can replicate. It's about perfecting the art then moving on to the next recipe.

The first time I made macarons was in the late 1990s when I was engrossed in Jacque Torres's book, Dessert Circus. The book had a recipe for macarons, but it was the old-fashioned variety that blended almond paste, sugar, and still-liquid egg whites.

Fast forward to 2013 when I began to see pictures and posts about macaron cookies and how finicky they were to make. I thought to myself, how difficult could they really be?

One of my weaknesses is following through with most of the ideas that happen to set up shop in my head. I do sufficient enough research, then throw caution to the wind and go for it. I used a volume-based recipe on *trial 1*. I was too lazy to measure everything; all I had to do was take the scale out of the kitchen drawer. Okay, that was a mistake. Though the discs had just a bit of a point in the middle, some baked up nicely while others were lopsided.

Trial 2 was picture perfect, using a recipe I found on eatlivetravelwrite.com. I measured all the ingredients using the Edlund scale I bought from Jacque Torres. The macarons had high feet and were somewhat hollow. I filled the chocolate macaron discs with Dove dark chocolate ganache and freshly grated coconut. They matured overnight and were deliciously chewy and soft in the morning. By the second day, the actual discs were too soft and they lost their chew.

Figure 7 - Chocolate macarons with dark chocolate ganache and freshly grated coconut

One day during the ensuing week, I signed up for a macaron class at A Southern Season in Chapel Hill, NC. I figured, however, that I should get another round or two of experience before the class.

I was tired of unrolling parchment paper so I bought flat sheets through an online baking store. I used it for *trial 3*. Good gosh, the macs deflated and did all kinds of crazy things; it was the exact recipe from the second attempt above. The lesson here was that yes, a change in baking parchment can spell disaster for macarons. They were edible, but I wanted perfection!

Figure 8 - Lopsided macs from a change in parchment paper

Moving on to *trial 4*, I tried a plain almond recipe from bravetart.com. The macs were pretty, but still somewhat hollow. The ones on the silicone mat kept their circular shape while the ones on parchment were not as perfectly round. I opted to fill the macs and keep them at room temperature overnight. The heart-wrenching lesson here was that filled macarons must be stored in the fridge or they'll become mush sitting on the counter at room temperature. I tested fate and lost.

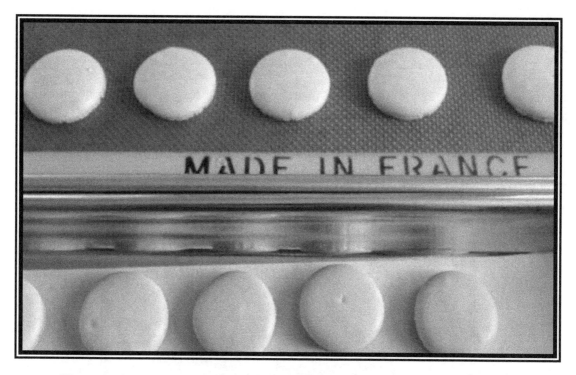

Figure 9 - Comparison of macarons on parchment paper compared to silicone mat

Thus far, I had managed to make pretty, but empty macaron discs. I was now more than ready to take the class and learn the secrets to making non-hollow macarons.

The macarons made by the pastry chef did not come out as perfect as I had hoped; there was still a bit of hollowness in the cookies and the tops sunk somewhat. On the other hand, knowing how temperamental these little devils can be, I chalked it up to someone else preparing the ingredients; different, somewhat-working ovens; liquid coloring; yadda, yadda, yadda. The chef also incorporated the basic meringue in three increments to the almond mixture. I asked why and his response was "so you don't get any lumps in the batter." He baked his cookies in a convection oven at 320 degrees Fahrenheit for 12 minutes. I did note that he used meringue powder for his Italian meringue, not his French meringue.

For ***trial 5*** I wanted to try my own recipe since I was not too confident in the results from the macaron class. I did more research and decided to use the ratios created by Ms. Humble. Again, I had a full batch of pretty but perfectly hollow macarons.

At this point, I read through all the notes I made over the last few weeks before venturing on to ***trial 6***. I decided that Chef Martin's recipe from class was the least hollow and the closest I had come to perfection in an actual macaron demonstration. I followed the recipe exactly, but beat the meringue and performed the macaronage the way I had been doing all along. I ended up with somewhat similar results to the macarons in class. The tops were too soft for my liking and I still had a hollow problem. I also tried the lower, middle, and upper levels of my oven as opposed to baking all the trays on the upper level.

Figure 10 - From left to right, trials 6, 7, 8, and 9

Moving right along, I took a small step back and thought about the chocolate macarons. The cocoa powder in the recipe—which is simply the plain recipe from bravetart.com with the addition of cocoa powder—must have something in it that kept the inside of the cookies from collapsing. Indeed, cocoa powder is a drying agent. Obviously, I didn't always want chocolate macarons. This begged the question, "What is white and has the same properties as cocoa powder?" I did my research and ran my next experiment.

Trial 7 consisted of the plain recipe from bravetart.com with the addition of 0.1 ounces of meringue powder, 1 teaspoon of red food coloring powder, and eggs aged two nights at room temperature. Most experiments test one variable at a time, but I decided that these three changes wouldn't hurt the cookies. By gosh, I should have perfect macarons ... or so I thought. Trial seven proved that I was on the right track, but still had a bit to go.

I was looking at eight rounds and realized that no recipe should take me eight attempts. This is not, after all, making pulled-sugar roses or crafting swans from blown sugar. I took a giant leap back. I reminded myself that I was working with a basic meringue, adding a dry mixture to the meringue, and baking it.

Ah, the light bulb. I pulled out one of my baking science books. I read all about meringues in BakeWise. In sum, meringues need stability to maintain their shape as they cook. That is, the meringue that I use must have plenty of holding power so that it does not collapse, thus solving my problem with hollow cookies. I had some experience with meringues already when I made my recipe for Coconut Cream Pie. I had used a cornstarch-water slurry, fresh and warmed eggs, moderate whipping, a hot filling, and a preheated pan.

For *trial 8*, I was not comfortable using the cornstarch-water slurry, so I opted for 1 tablespoon of flour and a bit of cream of tartar, using the bravetart.com plain recipe. I mixed in 3 teaspoons of vegetable oil to the store-bought almond flour per bravetart.com. Pretty, but flour is not a good option; it tasted off, and of course, the vegetable oil was one-too-many a variable. Oh that's right, they were still hollow.

I was excited to wake up the next morning for *trial 9* because I was going to use the egg whites I had aged for three nights in the fridge and one night at room temperature. I used Chef Martin's recipe, but added 2 teaspoons tapioca starch, ¼ teaspoon cream of tartar, and a combo of medium and high speed; I had been using high speed for trials one through eight. I also followed the chef's lead on incorporating the meringue into the almond mixture in small portions. Holy cow! I wish 320 degrees Fahrenheit was actually 320 degrees Fahrenheit in my oven because all of these macarons would have been almost perfect! The macs cooked at too high a heat had volcanoes—where the steam burst through the tops—but the meringue filled much of the cookie. The macs baked at lower temperatures were NOT hollow. Thank goodness, I was getting somewhere.

Figure 11 - Trial 9, using tapioca starch

If I was excited for trial nine, I couldn't contain myself for *trial 10*. Fresh eggs are better if the goal is a stable meringue as opposed to a high-volume meringue, or so I read. I warmed cold, fresh eggs in a bowl of 100-degree water for 10 minutes; dried, separated, and measured them;

and proceeded to make my meringue still using tapioca starch, cream of tartar, mostly medium whipping of the whites, and incremental macaronage. It took the piped batter about 1 ½ hours to develop a dry, hard crust, compared to all previous trials that took about 30 minutes. By the time I baked the last of the five trays, it had been drying for 3 hours. Needless to say, the feet of the macs were half the size, thus the discs themselves were very short; the first three trays were not hollow, but the last two trays were just as hollow as the non-starch trials. In sum, aged egg whites are a must simply for the macs to dry fast and get into the oven. I also watched my oven temperature very closely. It fluctuated 20 degrees from the temperature I set on the oven's dial. This was not good.

Figure 12 - Trial 10, tapioca starch and freshly cracked "fresh" eggs

I took a deep breath and assimilated all that I had learned so far. Ah, another light bulb. I'm pretty sure that every "do this not that" I had read about macarons on the Internet is the result of vastly different ovens. Because of this single variable, bakers and chefs swear by aged eggs, by resting the piped batter, and by some other tip. Keeping a preheated pan in my electrical oven was not enough to maintain a stable oven temperature. Instead of replacing my oven, I opted to buy a baking stone.

Trial 11 I think would have been perfect if the egg whites didn't lose so much water! Well, I also used an extra teaspoon of tapioca starch. I ended up with very thick dough; there was not enough meringue to make the batter more fluid. I piped a tray and almost tossed the whole darn batch. I realized quickly that I could smooth out the top with water, as some do—which I didn't think was a good trick because that's adding moisture to the shell—but the batch was a bust anyway, so it couldn't be any worse. The preheated baking stone helped, but just a little bit; I will continue to use it. The discs baked tall instead of wide; they had great feet though. Best of all, none were hollow. From this trial, I learned that I should take out about a ½ cup of the dry ingredients—after the almond flour and powdered sugar were mixed and sifted together—and set it aside. By doing this, I would ensure that whatever the volume the meringue whipped up to be—whatever amount of moisture was in the meringue—I would still be able to make a flowing batter.

Figure 13 - Trial 11, tapioca starch with fresh egg whites that were aged for two days at room temperature

I felt like I was closing in on the best macs ever, so I tackled *trial 12* while the macs from trial 11 were still baking. The problem was, however, that I didn't have any aged egg whites and the last of my almond flour was in my freezer. I thawed the flour on the counter and with a few bursts of heat in the microwave. No problems here, though the flour did look more moist than the flour from A Southern Season. I also decided that I would use the eggs that I had on my counter—which were still old—but not "aged." If it was a bust, well, at least I would know without a doubt that the egg whites must sit out for at least a day. The results were displeasing! The feet oozed around the perimeter of the first tray of macs. I decided I'd have to try the bottom rack of the oven as well as bake a few trays without the foil shield under the upper element. Ugh, I ended up with some macs hollow and some not.

Figure 14 - Trial 12, using an extra ounce of tapioca starch and freshly cracked, old egg whites

I reviewed trials 11 and 12. The failure of trial 11 could be that the egg whites lost so much moisture that their total volume decreased significantly by the time I made the meringue; the failure of trial 12 was that old eggs still had too much water. In preparation for trial 13, I weighed the whites of five eggs. The total weight of the egg whites I set out to age came to 5.2 ounces; I placed these whites at the same location in my dining room as I did for trial 11.

For lucky *trial 13*, I kept the temperature in my house the same as trial 11. I reweighed the egg whites again and guess what? The weight of the whites went from 5.2 ounces to 4.1 ounces in 48 hours! It's no wonder I did not have enough meringue for trial 11. I ran out of store-bought almond flour and had to grind my own; I ground it the same morning I made the macs. The flour looked moist. Otherwise, I kept the same recipe and techniques as described in both trials 11 and 12. No hollows on any of the trays! That was great ... except the surface of the shells were not cooked through and the feet oozed out on some of the macs. After taking the trays out of the oven and setting them on the stovetop, spots on the surface of the macs deflated; it may not have helped that it was a rainy day and the outside humidity was 72%.

I reviewed trial 12, where I had used home-ground almond flour out of the freezer; the feet oozed to the perimeter as well. It's safe to say, and according to foodnoveau.com, greasy or wet looking shells may be the result of oily or wet flour. I should have ground the flour ahead of time and dried it along with the egg whites. The surface problems could also be due to the fact that the ratio of caster sugar to egg whites is very low, at 38%. For trial 14, I'd buy the almond flour again and increase the caster sugar to 2.1 ounces instead of 1.5 ounces, for a ratio of about 51%.

Figure 15 - Trial 13, no hollows but blotchy due to freshly ground almond flour

Goodness me! *Trial 14* was two steps backward. Increasing the sugar totally upset the batter. I learn something new with every trial. With every trial, I get closer and closer to what works. Keeping on as a "mad scientist," I opted to immediately work on trial 15. Below is picture-proof of my evolution into a "mad scientist." I smashed all those darn cookies.

Figure 16 - Trial 14, adding more caster sugar

Trial 15 sent me back to happy-hollow-free-land. I did not have any aged eggs so I decided that this next experiment was still worth a shot. Some folks "age" their eggs in the microwave. I put five egg whites in the microwave and shot it with a couple of 8-second and 5-second bursts of power. I watched the weight disappear off the scale; it magically came back just before I made the meringue. I added another 0.1 ounces of tapioca starch just in case. The macs were all full, but small parts of the surface of the macs were collapsing in the oven; this made the tops somewhat wrinkled. I began to think that the tops were not getting enough heat. Thus, I removed the foil shield I had used throughout most of the trials—the upper heating element had been making the macs too dark. I only had one pan left to bake without the shield. Ah, it worked. The macs had great feet, smooth tops, full—but were so dark. Instead of yellow macs I had brown ones. Check them out below.

Figure 17 - Trial 15, eggs "aged" in the microwave

Egg whites must be aged, period! Aged egg whites have very low moisture. This permits the tops of the macs to set properly and the cookies themselves to cook completely in a short amount of time. The question became, "Are farm-fresh, high-stability, high-moisture, expensive eggs better than the old, low-stability, low-moisture, cheaper eggs? My recipe at this point is below and is what was used for trial 16:

4 ounces aged eggs

1.5 ounces caster sugar

5 ounces store-bought almond flour

8 ounces Domino's-brand powdered sugar

0.4 ounces tapioca starch

¼ teaspoon cream of tartar

½ teaspoon powdered food coloring or 4 drops gel coloring

Trial 16 was a success! Okay, it was not as perfect as I wanted it to be, but I chalk that up to my oven's heat. While it is only six years old, it's been through the ringer. I tested the middle and lower racks, different temperatures, a dark pan, an unheated nesting pan, and a preheated nesting pan. After reviewing that data, I'm going to stick with 310 degrees Fahrenheit, an unheated nesting pan, using the lower rack of my oven, pushing the pans all the way in to about 2 to 3 inches from the back of the oven, and of course keeping the baking stone in there as the oven preheats. I also noticed that for the last pan in, the macs baked somewhat lopsided; this could be because it was about 2 hours and 15 minutes since I piped the batter. It took a while to bake the five pans because I had changed the temperature and gave the oven 5 minutes between sheets to level out its heat.

Figure 18 - Trial 16, nearly perfect though some collapsed a tiny bit in the middle

I hoped trial 17 would give me picture-perfect macs. I'd increase tapioca starch a tad to 0.5 ounces instead of 0.4 ounces. I'd also test whether or not farm-fresh, aged eggs were better than old, aged eggs.

Trial 17 was successful because I cracked the oven door open a little bit using a wooden rice cooker spoon. Cracking the door open enabled the moisture to evaporate out of the oven, setting the top of the macs so they did not collapse at all. I also used a small fan to blow a gentle breeze across the macs while they were drying. In my opinion, farm-fresh eggs did not make a difference. My only problem with this round was that I had to bake the last two trays of the macs at 315 degrees Fahrenheit; they were a tad too brown for me. The picture below includes the green macs from trial 16.

Figure 19 - Filled macs from trials 16 and 17

For trial 18, I would use old eggs that had been aged for three days. And I'd try baking at 310 degrees Fahrenheit to see if it minimized browning while still cooking the macs properly. This time, I had five trays instead of four.

Trial 18 netted the "perfect" macaron. The three-day old eggs were much thicker than the two-day old eggs. The rate of moisture loss dropped by one-tenth of an ounce to 0.4 ounces per day; this is probably because I aged a greater total volume of whites for three days as opposed to a smaller total volume of whites for two days. Fortunately, I had been keeping a very detailed record of my trials, so I was able to go back and compare the baking duration and temperature for trials 16, 17, and 18. These experiments were practically identical, but I was able to identify a few key points concerning baking macs in my oven: (1) if I set my oven's dial to 310 degrees Fahrenheit, the temperature at the front, left corner fluctuates between 285ish and 325ish degrees Fahrenheit, but settled at about 300 degrees; (2) if I set the dial to 315 degrees, the temperature never falls below 305ish and doesn't exceed 335ish degrees, but settles at predominantly 305 degrees; (3) and at 315 degrees on the oven's dial for trials 17 and 18, the duration of baking dropped from 19 minutes to 17 minutes. The conclusion I was able to draw from all three comparisons was that aging the egg whites sets the tops of the macs quickly, thus reducing the baking time. The end result is barely browned, beautiful macaron discs!

I was supposed to do trial 19 with four-day old eggs, but I decided to wait another day to test five-day old eggs since the egg whites don't appear to have any foul odor. I'm hypothesizing that if the difference between two-day and three-day old egg whites reduced baking time by 2 minutes, then another two days will reduce the duration by enough time to minimize browning even more. If my hypothesis proves to be correct, the good news is that you can make beautiful, full macs using whites that you've aged for three to five days.

Trial 19, using five-day old eggs, yielded very dense macs! The "dough" inside the cookies stuck to the underside of the tops like glue; these macs were not just full, but filled to the brim. On the other hand, the macs did not spread out as much and baked to a smaller diameter. My oven decided to misbehave and fell shy of 300 degrees Fahrenheit a few times. It still took 17 minutes for the macs to cook; my hypothesis proved incorrect. I actually preferred my recipe with three-day old eggs. However, I now knew that if I had to age the eggs another two days it would not be a big deal! Also, the volume of egg whites went from 6.8 ounces to 4.3 ounces, a loss of 2.5 ounces over five days, or 0.5 ounces per day. If you are aging your eggs for five days, be sure you have an extra 2.5 or so ounces of egg whites. In my video, I used five-day old eggs, but followed the exact process as trial 18, which used three-day old eggs. These little morsels, hundreds of them literally, gave me the challenge I had been yearning for. It was a challenge that I craved, a challenge that I had not been able to find under the heavy barbells for three years now. I beat you, you "finicky" schmucks!

RECIPES

I have been baking since grade school. Several years ago I simply got tired of trying to find my place in a recipe—where did I leave off in the list of ingredients; where am I in all the steps. As such, I've developed a less traditional format for writing my recipes to make preparation and reading more efficient.

I use "Sets" to distinguish the components of a recipe that must stand alone, or for ingredients that can be mixed together. For example, because the egg whites must be aged ahead of time, I list them by themselves under "Set 1." Since the almond flour and powdered sugar go together, they are listed under "Set 2."

Generally, I include a list of tools at the beginning of a recipe. However, because the production of the finished macaron cookies is multi-step, I've listed the tools you need under the specific ingredients and tasks.

For Kindle formatting purposes, I have omitted the numbers from the directions.

The best way to approach these recipes is to read them in their entirety then go through and highlight all the things you need in your specific kitchen to make the macaron discs and your choice of fillings.

Macaron Discs

PaulaQ's French Macarons

Because I wanted to write this recipe as a stand-alone recipe, I did replicate a few key sections from the body of this book.

Makes 112 discs, or 56 filled macaron cookies

Modern macaron—ma-ka-rohn—cookies, not to be confused with coconut macaroon, are basically two discs of nutty meringue that sandwich a sweet filling. A meringue is basically egg whites whipped with sugar. French meringue, also called basic meringue, is the easiest though most delicate style of making meringue; it blends sugar into room temperature egg whites. This recipe uses the French meringue method for making macarons.

There are many tools you will need for this recipe. The most important are the kitchen scale and the oven thermometer. My electric scale happens to measure in grams and ounces. However, the gram measurement is in multiples of 2 grams, while the ounce measurement reads into the tenth place. Using ounces, I can get a little more exact. I check the accuracy of my scale using a 1-pound box of powdered sugar. After owning it for more than 12 years, I'm thrilled it's still working perfectly!

The heat in the oven sets the structure of the meringue and gives the macarons their characteristic feet. The amount of heat and the rate of heat application are vital for perfect macarons, and they can potentially be the most unstable aspect of making macarons. Without a convection oven, you must create an extremely stable meringue and quickly apply as much constant heat to your cookies as you can without burning them. The heat creates the feet and holds the meringue in place so the macarons don't become hollow. I have an electric oven without a convection feature.

I use a 4.5 quart Kitchen Aid stand mixer; the mixing time below refers to this specific machine. You can certainly use another brand or even a hand beater, but be sure to beat the meringue until it is stiff. If your mixer is very old or very new, the settings could run slightly slower or faster than my Kitchen Aid.

Do your prep work two days before you will make the macaron discs. All measurements are in weight, not in volume, including the egg whites.

Be sure to watch my video on YouTube.com, "The ULTIMATE French Macaron Recipe Using French Meringue," before reading too far into this recipe, and certainly before attempting to make the cookies. The video demonstrates that these cookies are not so difficult to make, and they are less time-consuming compared to making guyuria, a Guam cookie. My recipe was inspired by pastry chef Martin Brunner of The Bakehouse in Aberdeen, North Carolina.

I have to tell you how much I appreciate all of the fraction, decimal, and percentage exercises that I had to do in my math classes as I was creating this recipe. Kudos to all my math teachers!

I've written these directions with as much detail as possible for this specific recipe using my electric oven and an old Kitchen Aid mixer. Though my recipe is quite detailed, delicious and beautiful macs also depend on your specific oven. You may have to make this recipe two or three times simply to get the macs perfect in your very own oven.

INGREDIENTS

Set 1

6.0 to 6.3 ounces egg whites*

You will ultimately use only 4 ounces of three-day old whites (4 oz. = 113.40 g / 6.0 oz. = 170.10 g / 6.3 oz. = 178.60 g).

*If aging the eggs for five days, you'll need 6.8 ounces, or 192.78 grams, of whites to start with.

Set 2

5 ounces almond flour/meal (141.75 grams)

8 ounces powdered sugar (226.80 grams)

Set 3

1.5 ounces caster sugar (42.52 grams)

0.5 ounces tapioca starch (14.18 grams)

¼ teaspoon cream of tartar

Set 4

½ teaspoon powdered food coloring or 4 to 5 drops gel coloring

Day 1

Egg Whites: 6 to 6.3 ounces of egg whites, the whites from six large eggs (if aging for five days, start with about 6.8 ounces)

Tools: two cereal bowls, kitchen scale

Use the uncracked eggs that you have had on your counter or in your fridge for a couple of days.

Turn your scale on if it's electrical. Place one bowl on the scale then tare the scale or set it to zero.

Separate one egg over one bowl. If you did not break the yolk, pour the single egg white into the bowl on the scale; if you broke the yolk, save the egg for scrambled eggs. Wash and dry your bowl then start all over. Repeat this process until you have measured about 6 ounces of egg whites.

Leave the bowl of whites at room temperature—about 72 degrees Fahrenheit—uncovered, for three days on your counter. If there are bugs flying around, cover the entire container with a sheet of cheesecloth.

Almonds: 5 ounces store-bought almond flour or 6 ounces home-ground almond flour

It's best to use store-bought almond flour if this is your first time. Simply measure out 5 ounces of store-bought almond flour into a container with a cover. Cover the flour and set aside until ready to use.

If you do not have store-bought almond flour, here is how you can grind your own.

Tools: coffee grinder, fine-mesh strainer, medium bowl, adult dinner spoon, kitchen scale, 2-cup container with cover

Note on the strainer: The holes of the strainer must be tiny. The holes should measure less 1/16 of an inch. A small thumbtack would not be able to fit through the hole. This is essential otherwise you end up with very bumpy surfaces on your baked macarons.

Place the 2-cup container on the scale then set the scale to zero.

Grab a handful of blanched, slivered almonds and place the nuts into a clean coffee grinder that you use just for spices or nuts. Grind at the fine setting for 5 to 8 seconds, shaking the coffee grinder to shake up the nuts as they grind. If you grind too long, the nuts will turn into nut butter. You can sift a piece or two of caked up nut butter, but not the entire batch.

Pour the ground nuts into a fine-mesh strainer set atop a medium bowl. Use the adult dinner spoon to push-and-stir the nuts through the mesh. The small pieces will go through easily while some pieces may take a bit of effort.

Spoon the "large" pieces back into the grinder.

Pour the finely sieved nuts into the 2-cup container on the scale.

Add another handful of nuts to the coffee grinder and repeat the entire process until you have measured 6 ounces of finely ground almonds.

Leave the flour uncovered in your kitchen until it's ready to use in a few days.

If the flour still looks moist or wet, you will have to dry it in your oven at 200 degrees Fahrenheit for 30 minutes. Cool the flour completely before using.

Sugars: 1.5 ounces caster sugar, and 8 ounces powdered sugar

Tools: 1-cup container with cover, 2-cup container with cover

Since you have your scale out, measure the caster sugar into the 1-cup container as described above. Do the same for the powdered sugar using the 2-cup container. Cover the containers and set aside.

Note: The crystal sizes of caster sugar are absolutely much smaller than even the superfine table sugar many grocers carry. Some folks place table sugar into a blender and process the sugar into smaller particles. If you are unable to get caster sugar, this can be done as an alternative.

Prepare Your Parchment Patterns

Tools: 5 high-quality or professional half-sheet pans, 1 to 5 silicone mats, parchment paper, circle patterns, pencil, clean cooling racks, kitchen towels, Microsoft Word or other word processor, printer

Wash your silicone mats in warm water using a soft sponge. Dry thoroughly with a kitchen towel and place on clean cooling racks to dry completely.

If you are not adept at manually piping even circles of batter, use a pattern:

Open a blank Word document then insert a circle. You'll have to adjust the size, print the document, and then readjust the size of the circle back on your computer until you get a circle that measures about 1 1/16 to 1 1/8 of an inch in diameter. A diameter is the distance across opposite sides of a circle, running through the middle.

Copy and paste the circle so you end up with three circles in a horizontal line, as straight as possible; space them evenly. Select two circles then copy and paste them below the first row. Stagger the row of two circles such that the circles are between the three circles above.

Copy and paste the rows so you end up with five, alternating, staggered rows of circles. Print one sheet.

Lay the sheet on the baking pan then put a piece of parchment over them, wrong side up. Align the left sides of the pattern and the parchment together if you are a right-handed person; align the right sides if you are a lefty. Instead of tracing each circle in its entirety, mark only the top, bottom, and side borders of each circle with a dash. When you pipe the batter with your bag perpendicular to the parchment, the batter will spread in a circle; stop when you hit the marked borders.

Begin your tracings from left to right if you are a righty so you don't smear pencil markings all over the place; work right to left if you are a lefty. Set aside until day four.

Note: I tear out sheets of parchment from my roll and lay them flat for several weeks so they are ready to use as needed.

Prep the Piping Bags

Tools: two 12-inch cake decorating or piping bags, 2 sets of couplers, #12 Wilton round tip or a tip that measures 5/16 of an inch in diameter, #10 Wilton round tip or a tip that measures 3/16 to ¼ of an inch in diameter, plastic wrap

Cut a small piece off the tip of one piping bag so that when you place the long part of the coupler—called the base—narrow end in first, the edge lines up with the cut-end of the bag; the coupler can be slightly shy of the opening.

Place the #12 tip over the base then attach the ring to secure the tip in place. This bag will be used to pipe the macaron batter.

Repeat for tip #10; this will be used for the filling. Set aside.

Days 2 and 3 (days 4 and 5 as well if aging eggs for five days)

Do nothing.

Day 4 (or Day 6 if aging whites for five days)

Clean the Meringue Tools

Tools: stand mixer with bowl and whisk attachment, 4-cup measuring pitcher, small plate, rubber spatula, clean kitchen towels or paper towels

Boil 4 cups of water in the microwave using a measuring pitcher.

Set the mixer bowl on the counter. Hold the whisk over the mixing bowl in one hand as you pour some of the boiling water over the whisk. Dry the whisk thoroughly then attach to the mixer.

Repeat with the small plate. Dry thoroughly.

Clean the spatula with boiling water, again over the mixing bowl. Pour the water out. Dry and set the spatula on the clean plate.

Carefully whirl the hot water around the entire inner surface of the mixing bowl. Dry thoroughly. The tools will cool off while you work on the next step.

Note: After so many trials, I stopped doing all this because I was using the tools just for the meringue! I ensured that after I used soapy water to clean the meringue-dirtied tools, I rinsed them in very hot water. If you use the same bowls and beaters to make anything with butter, Crisco, or oil, do this cleaning step every time.

Prepare Your Baking Pans

Tools: 5 high-quality or professional half-sheet pans, 1 to 5 silicone mats and/or prepared parchment paper, non-stick spray if using parchment

If using parchment, spray the pan with non-stick spray.

Turn the parchment right side up. Carefully apply the parchment paper to the prepared pan as if applying tint to a window or wallpaper to a wall.

If using silicone mats, lay the mats flat on your pans.

Mix Almond Flour with Powdered Sugar

Tools: large food processor, fine-mesh strainer, medium bowl, large stainless-steel mixing bowl, adult dinner spoon

Pour the almond flour that you sifted yesterday into the bowl of the food processor.

Add the powdered sugar to the same bowl.

Cover the bowl and give it a couple of pulses. Uncover and use the spoon to scrape any unmixed parts at the bottom and edges of the food processor bowl.

Give it a few more whirls. Uncover and remove the bowl from the food processor. Move the processor out of your way.

Situate the strainer atop the medium bowl. Spoon some of the almond flour-powdered sugar mixture into the strainer. Use the spoon to sift the mixture.

Repeat until you have sieved it all. Carefully pour the dry mixture into the large stainless steel bowl.

Reserve a ½ cup of the almond flour and powdered sugar mixture. Do this by taking an adult dinner spoon and pouring the mixture over the ½-cup measuring cup. Use a straight edge knife to flatten the surface of the mixture in the cup. Set aside.

Note: I have never needed to use all of the dry ingredients in this recipe. Once I am done piping the batter, I pour this dry mix into a separate container. When I have 13 ounces of proportionately correct flour and sugar, I will try using it in this same recipe—in lieu of measuring out the almond flour and powdered sugar again. I'll post updates on this particular trial to my website.

Set your baking pans and piping bags up in the area that you are going to pipe your macaron batter.

Preheat Your Oven

Tools: 2 oven racks, oven thermometer, baking stone

Place one oven rack at the lowest level of your oven. Set the baking stone on the rack. Place your oven thermometer on the same rack, to the front and left corner, where you can read it easily with the oven door closed and the oven light turned on. It should not be in the way when you insert and remove your baking pans.

Keep your oven light turned on. Set the heat dial of your oven to 250 degrees Fahrenheit and allow to preheat as you make your batter, keeping the oven door slightly ajar to dry the air in your kitchen.

Reweigh the Egg Whites

Use your scale and a clean bowl to measure out exactly 4 ounces of egg whites from the egg whites that you have been aging. Leave the scale out for the next step below.

Make the French Meringue

Tools: cleaned stand mixer tools

Place your container of caster sugar on the scale and tare it to zero. **Add 0.5 ounces of tapioca starch** to the sugar. Add ¼ teaspoon of cream of tartar to the sugar. Stir to combine thoroughly. Put your scale away.

Pour the egg whites and the sugar mixture into the bowl of your mixer; use a clean spatula or clean fingers to scrape as much of the whites as you can into the mixer bowl. Use the mixer's beater to somewhat stir the dry ingredients by hand into the egg whites for only 3 seconds; this reduces the amount of powder that mists into the air once you turn the mixer on. Attach the beater to the mixer and secure the mixer bowl; lock the mixer in place.

Beat the egg whites and sugar at medium speed for 6 minutes; medium is number 4 for the Kitchen Aid. I use my microwave's digital timer. At the end of 6 total minutes of whipping at level 4, you will have a very soft-peaked meringue.

Turn the speed to medium-high—that's number 5 on the Kitchen Aid. Beat for 9 minutes. At the end of this stage, you will have a stiff meringue at the early stage of stiff peaks. Stop the mixer and remove the beater. Dip the beater into the meringue, and note how it feels.

Add a ½ teaspoon of powdered food coloring or 4 drops of gel coloring; incorporate the color somewhat using the beater.

Attach the beater and turn the speed to high; that's number 6 on the Kitchen Aid. Beat for 1 minute.

Macaronage

Tools: cleaned rubber spatula, 2 small spoons, small bowl, kitchen towel, ½-cup measuring cup, straight-edge knife or cake decorating spatula

Unlock your mixer and remove the bowl. Detach the whisk and shake the meringue back into the mixer bowl. Set the mixer aside and out of your way.

Scoop half of the meringue out of the whipping bowl and thoroughly incorporate it into the dry mixture; do this by folding the batter onto itself and pressing the batter against the sides and bottom of the bowl; it's not a matter of being gentle or rough, just being thorough. Once the mixtures are well mixed, lift some batter up with the spatula then let it fall back into the bowl. Look at your batter closely; it will look pretty thick. Add a small portion of the remaining meringue. Incorporate well again. Look at your batter; it should look thinner, with the ribbons slowly blending into the surrounding batter. Add the last of the meringue and tenderly fold it in—now is the time to be gentle. Incorporate thoroughly. Test the batter by scooping a small amount of batter out of the bowl with a small cereal spoon. Ladle the batter into a mound in a plastic bowl, trailing the batter on the top to mimic the point of a piped macaron. Tap the plate on the counter. If the tip disappears, your batter is ready. If not, return the batter to the bowl and fold 10 more strokes. Test again.

Once your batter is ready, lay a sheet of plastic wrap out on the counter next to you. Use your spatula to scoop batter onto the sheet at a diagonal; the ends of the mound of batter should point to opposite ends of the plastic wrap. Fold the lower half of the plastic over the mound of batter and smooth it over the mound. Twist the ends and tuck the ends under the mound. Repeat with remaining batter, making three wrapped mounds.

Note: The batter will spread a little bit as you do this; that's okay. Fold the lower half of the batter onto the upper half of the batter when you fold the plastic wrap; it's like folding a tortilla to make a soft taco.

Pipe Your Batter

Clip one end of a wrapped mound of batter. Squeeze a bit of batter to the open end and insert this end into the prepared piping bag. Shake the bag to shimmy the wrapped batter to the piping end.

Twist the piping bag to hold the bag comfortably in your hand and to keep the batter in place.

Pipe your batter onto your prepared parchment patterns or on the silicone mats. Keep the piping tip about one-eighth of an inch from the pan; this will pop some of the bubbles as you squeeze the batter out.

If you are using silicone mats or didn't make a pattern on the parchment papers, try this technique to pipe even circles:

Say aloud for every circle, **"One, two, three."** Lift the tip up immediately after "three" and hover just above the mound for 1 second then quickly move over about 1 ½ to 2 inches and repeat, **"One, two, three,"** lift, hover, and move over. Repeat to fill up the pan. Apply even pressure on the bag for all the circles. Let the trailing tip of icing fall onto the circle you just finished piping then quickly move over to make the next circle. The batter is thin so it will start to ooze out of the tip as soon as you finish piping. However, it's thick enough so that you have enough time to quickly move on.

Tap Your Pan

Tools: toothpicks, small fan

Once you have piped all your circles, set the piping bag aside, ensuring the tip is higher than the rest of the bag.

Hold on to each short side of the pan then gently hit the pan against the counter 8 times to bring the air bubbles to the top. Quickly prick the bubbles with a clean, sharp toothpick. Go back over the piped batter and prick the bubbles again; it should not take you more than 1 minute to pop the bubbles. More bubbles will come up, but leave them alone after 1 minute. If you wait too long to pop the bubbles, or if you try to pop all the bubbles that come up, the crust will start to form and the pricks will show on your finished, baked macs.

Set this pan aside and let it dry for 50 to 60 minutes. Position a small, desktop fan across from your trays such that there is a gentle breeze wafting across the piped batter. The goal of drying really is to allow the batter to form a dry, hard crust. The duration depends on the humidity in your kitchen. Use the first pan as your gauge. Once the macs on the first pan have crusted, start baking.

Repeat the piping, tapping, popping, and drying for the remaining pans.

Bake 'em up

Tools: several cooling racks, two extra AND exact baking pans, wooden rice scooper spoon

While your macs are drying, check the temperature in your oven. Though you may have set the oven's dial to 315 degrees Fahrenheit, the temperature at the location of your thermometer may be different. Just make a note so you know how your oven is behaving. If you are using parchment paper instead of silicone macs, you need to reduce the oven temperature to about 300 or 305 degrees Fahrenheit and see what happens; macs cook too quickly on parchment paper at the higher temperature! At too high of a heat the feet will ooze out.

Nest one tray of macs into another tray of the exact same size. Place these nested trays on top of the baking stone and push the trays into the oven until they are about 3 inches from the back wall. Close the oven's door and shimmy a thin spoon, like a rice cooker spoon, between the door and the oven, about 1/3 of the way down the side; this aids in setting and drying the tops of the macs. You should be able to see a ¼-inch crack of space at the side of the oven. **Bake for 16 minutes.**

Open the oven door and push on the top of one of the macarons. If it does not move, the cookies are done. If it moves, bake for another minute then check for doneness again.

Remove the pan from the oven and place on a cooling rack. Cool completely then remove the macaron discs.

As you continue to bake, opening and closing the oven door, the temperature will fluctuate a bit. Set your timer for 2 minutes every time you take out a try. This gives your oven some time to correct its temperature. Be sure to check your temperature, waiting if necessary for it to get close to its own inside, "normal" temperature … whatever it is when you set the oven's dial to 315 degrees Fahrenheit.

The macs may seem hard and crunchy by the time they are cooled, but they will soften and become chewy 12 to 48 hours after they have been filled.

Note: Unfortunately, my electric oven may behave differently from your oven. You may have to slightly increase the temperature on the oven's dial if your macarons seem like they are not cooked within 16 to 18 minutes. If the macs are browning too much, place a foil shield under the upper element and see how it affects the macs. I found that in my oven, using a foil shield prevented the top of the macs from setting properly.

Maturing and Storing

Tools: several air-tight containers

Okay. Go right ahead and enjoy a couple of macaron discs. They are probably crunchy and hard; some might be soft and chewy. Regardless of whether you like them or not, they will taste better the next day after they have had time to soak up some of the moisture from the filling.

Unfilled

Arrange the unfilled discs in a single layer in freezer-gallon bags. Fill several bags and gently stack them in a covered container for up to five days. By the fifth day, you should place the container in the freezer to keep for several months.

Filled

They must be filled and matured to transform into the soft, chewy, sweet-filled cookies you know as French macarons. Here's the deal. If you use a hard filling—filling that stays quite firm at room temperature—then you can fill the macs today and store them in the fridge; they will be ready to eat in 48 to 72 hours. However, if you use a soft filling, the macarons may be filled and kept in the fridge less, ready in 12 to 24 hours. Maturation is something you will have to experiment with depending on how thick your discs and fillings are, and how much moisture is in each type of filling.

Filling the Macs

Tools: wrapped filling, prepared piping bag, kitchen scissors

Arrange your macaron discs in pairs of the same size and shape. Flip the bottom disc of the pair upside-down.

Clip one end of a wrapped mound of filling. Squeeze a bit of filling to the open end and insert this end into the prepared piping bag. Shake the bag to shimmy the wrapped filling to the piping end.

Twist the piping bag to hold the bag comfortably in your hand and to keep the filling in place.

Pipe enough filling onto the center of the flipped discs so that when you sandwich the filling, it's just under ¼-inch thick.

Note: I've discovered that fillings like lemon curd and jam are best at about a 1/8-inch thickness while cream cheese fillings are excellent closer to ¼-inch thick.

Hard Fillings

Dark Chocolate Ganache, Coconut optional

This recipe was adapted from davidlebovitz.com.

INGREDIENTS

Set 1

½ cup heavy cream

2 teaspoons light corn syrup or honey

Set 2

4 ounces Dove dark chocolate (or 15 square pieces)

¼ teaspoon instant espresso powder

Set 3

1 tablespoon unsalted butter, cut into small cubes

Set 4

½ to ¾ cup grated, fresh coconut

Note: Honey does have its own flavor, especially if it's from certain flowers like sage or wildflowers. The butter and the syrups enhance the shine and mouthfeel of the ganache.

Tools: 1-cup microwavable measuring pitcher, microwave oven, small whisk, medium bowl, rubber spatula, cutting board, knife, plastic wrap

DIRECTIONS

Chop the chocolate into very small pieces.

Use the pitcher to heat the heavy cream and corn syrup in the microwave just until it simmers.

Dissolve the espresso powder in the milk.

Pour the hot cream over the chopped chocolate and let stand for 2 minutes.

Use the small whisk to combine the ingredients until the chocolate is very smooth.

Add the small pieces of butter and stir to combine. Set aside, uncovered, until the ganache is cooled completely; the ganache will become quite firm.

Once the ganache is cooled and firm, wrap with plastic wrap just like you did for the macaron batter.

This hard filling may be piped immediately. It also keeps well in the fridge; however you have to set it out for an hour to come to room temperature or heat in microwave for 5 seconds—remove the metal tip first.

If you want to add coconut, pipe the ganache onto one macaron disc then sprinkle freshly grated coconut over the ganache. Gently press the second disc on the chocolate-and-coconut filling.

Note: Natural food stores sell unsweetened, dried coconut that you may use in place of the fresh coconut. Obviously, there will be a slight difference in texture and taste. Sometimes I mix the coconut directly into the chocolate so there is more coconut in each meringue. Occasionally I double batch the chocolate then use half for the coconut filling; I'll save the other half for plain chocolate.

Lemon Curd

This recipe was adapted from growitcookitcanit.com.

INGREDIENTS

Set 1

1 packed tablespoon of lemon zest

2 ½ cup granulated sugar

Set 2

4 large, whole eggs

8 egg yolks

Set 3

1 cup freshly squeezed lemon juice

¾ cup unsalted, cold butter, cubed into small pieces

Tools: small bowl; medium bowl; whisk; medium pot about 3.5 inches deep; large stainless steel bowl; strainer; rubber spatula; 4 freezer-safe, half-pint glass or plastic canning jars with lids and rings, cleaned but not sterilized; funnel

DIRECTIONS

Place the strainer over the medium bowl and set aside.

Fill the medium pot with enough water—about 1.5 inches. When you place the stainless steel bowl on top of the pot, the bottom of the bowl should not touch the water. Remove the stainless steel bowl from the pot. Turn the heat to half way between medium-low and medium (roughly the 8 o'clock position on your dial). Bring the water to a simmer.

Place the sugar and lemon zest in the small bowl. Stir to combine then set aside.

Put the whole eggs and the egg yolks into the stainless steel bowl. Whisk the eggs thoroughly until the mixture is light yellow and fluffy.

Add the sugar mixture to the eggs and blend well.

Add the lemon juice and whisk to combine.

Add the butter pieces.

Position the stainless steel bowl atop the pot of simmering water.

Use the rubber spatula to distribute the butter and stir the mixture.

Continue to stir the mixture until it reaches 170 degrees Fahrenheit. At this temperature, the curd will be thick like runny pancake batter. This takes about 25 minutes of stirring over simmering water. Don't turn the heat up or you might curdle the eggs. However, even at a low heat, you may see a few flecks of white, hardened egg whites. Don't worry about it because you will strain it out.

Once the curd is at 170 degrees Fahrenheit, pour it into the strainer. You can certainly save the strained zest and enjoy it over toast.

Place a funnel over one jar then pour enough curd into it, leaving half an inch of space from the top of the jar. Cover the jar with a lid and seal with the ring. Repeat with remaining jars.

Cool the jars completely at room temperature. Place in fridge overnight. Once cold, you can store the curd in the freezer. Thaw in fridge when ready to use.

The curd I keep in my fridge has lasted two weeks and still seems to be good.

Note: You may fill macarons with lemon curd, or mix the lemon curd into the cream cheese filling as described in "Soft Fillings" below.

Mango and Habanero Jam

I love fresh mango, so I thought I'd give spicy mango jam a try.

When buying your pectin, be sure it is the regular, or classic, not the reduced-sugar pectin. If you are buying a water or pressure canning pot, read the box; flat or glass-top ranges need pots specifically made for them. Also, use a pot that leaves you enough room to remove the cover; if you get one too big, it may also be too high. My pot is 16 quarts. It fits 8 half-pint jars.

The jars ard rings may be reused to make more jam; however, you will need to buy new lids.

I bought my canner at Wal-Mart. The tools I use to make jam came from kitchenkrafts.com; such tools were selected individually as there was no set.

Watch my how-to video, "strawberry JALAPENO jam," for a comprehensive demo on how to make jam. The video is available on YouTube.com, and at paulaq.com under the "More Recipes" tab. Substitute the mango-habanero recipe for the strawberry-jalapeno ingredients. Note there is a slight difference in one of the steps in the video.

To help ease the process of making jam, I buy, clean, cube, and freeze—or smash—and measure the fruits and peppers ahead of time. When I am ready to make jam, I simply thaw out the premeasured fruits and peppers overnight. I've made sweet pineapple, strawberry-jalapeno, blueberry, and raspberry jams following the exact process. However, depending on the specific fruit, the volume of ingredients is slightly different. For my other jam recipes, visit paulaq.com. Click on "More Recipes" at the top of the site; scroll down the page for the link to specific recipes.

INGREDIENTS

Set 1

7 cups cubed, ripe mango, not overripe (discard the skin and seeds then cut about ¾ inch cubes)

¼ cup somewhat packed, chopped orange habaneros, seeds and stems removed (use gloves)

¼ cup fresh lemon juice

½ cup water

2.5 ounces dry powdered fruit pectin (roughly equivalent to 7 tablespoons of Ball's powdered pectin in the plastic bottle)

Set 2

6 cups granulated sugar

Tools: food-safe gloves, canning pot with rack, jar lifter, lid lifter and bubble remover tool, jam funnel, large pot, small pot, immersion blender, two small plates, small spoon, large wooden spoon, 4 kitchen towels, plenty of napkins, heavy duty baking sheet, cooling rack, 4-cup measuring pitcher, trivet, 1-cup measuring cup

DIRECTIONS

Prepare Your Canning Supplies

Wash jars with soap and water; rinse well. Place jars, open side up, on the rack in a large pot for boiling-water canning. Fill the pot with water to a level about 1 inch above the top of the jars. Place the pot on the large burner on the left side of the stove. Cover and bring to a boil for 5 minutes; start the timer once you hear the water is at a rolling boil; a rolling boil is one in which the bubbles cannot be stirred away. It will take a while for the large amount of water to come to a boil.

While waiting for the water to boil, wash lids and rings in soapy water; rinse well. Place the lids only in a small pot and cover with water to a level about 1 inch above the lids. Set on a small burner on your stove.

Dry the rings and set aside.

Wash and dry your jar lifter, colander, and magnetic lid lifter/bubble remover.

Be sure you have several kitchen towels ready to set on your counter; you do not want to put hot jars of jam on a cold surface.

Make the Jam … While the Pot of Jars is Heating to a Boil

Heat the pot of lids to a gentle simmer just before you begin mixing the jam ingredients. Keep the lids at a low simmer. Do not boil the lids or they may not seal properly.

Place the mango, lemon juice, water, and habanero in a large pot. Stir with a wooden spoon to mix.

Use the immersion blender to pulverize the fruit and pepper slightly.

Sprinkle the pectin over the mixture and stir well.

Use the immersion blender to completely pulverize the ingredients in the pot.

Keep a trivet on your counter where you will put the cooked jam.

Put the pot of jam on the burner, on the right side of the stove, at medium heat. Bring to a boil, stirring constantly. Once the jam boils, stir in the sugar.

When it comes back to a rolling boil, cook for 1 minute.

Leave this burner turned on, but move the pot of jam to your counter, immediately to the right of the stove (if possible).

Putting it All Together

Take the pot of lids off the stove too.

Carefully move the boiling jars to the burner on the right; remember to keep this burner turn on, at medium heat.

Place the pot of lids on the left side of the stove on medium-low heat.

Carefully remove the lid of the pot with the jars; set the lid aside for now.

Use the jar lifter to pick up one jar, draining the water.

Place the sterile jar on the towel near your pot of jam then put the funnel on the jar.

Scoop 1 cup of jam into the funnel. Remove the funnel.

The jam should come up to ¼-inch from the top of the jar. Run the bubble remover along the sides of the jam or jar, releasing any bubbles. Use a small spoon to fill jam back to ¼-inch to 1/8-inch from the top.

Use a slightly moist napkin to clean the top and sides of the jar's rim, wiping off all traces of jam.

Take a lid from the pot using the lid lifter, shaking off some water. Place the lid on the rim.

Grab a ring then secure over the lid; tighten only with your fingers, not your entire palm. Set the jar aside on a towel-lined, heavy-duty baking sheet.

Repeat with remaining jars.

Once done, use the jar lifter to place all jars back into the pot of hot water. Ensure there is space between jars and from the perimeter of the pot.

Cover the pot, turn the heat up to medium-high, and then wait for the water to come to a rolling boil; you should be able to hear this.

At a rolling boil, set the timer for 10 minutes.

Turn the heat off then carefully uncover the pot. Use a jar lifter to take one jar of jam out of the pot at a time; tip the jar slightly, emptying the water on the lid.

Set all jars aside overnight to cool completely.

Once Cooled Completely

Press down on the top center of the lid of each jar. If you hear a clicking sound, the jar did not seal properly. Place unsealed jars in the fridge to eat first.

Unscrew only the ring of each sealed jar. Gently, but thoroughly, clean the rim and rings with a lightly damp cloth then dry with a dry cloth. Do not remove the lid or you will break the seal.

Screw the rings back on each jar.

Label all sealed jars with the flavor and date. Keep in a dark place for six to nine months for best results.

Soft Fillings

Mango and Cream

I love the combination of this filling with almond macs that are sprinkled with Himalayan pink salt. Brush some melted white Crisco on the surface of the baked and cooled macs then sprinkle with pink salt. Let dry and fill your macs. This filling matures the macaron discs in 18 to 24 hours. It loses its chewiness and becomes creamy-soft not long after 24 to 30 hours.

INGREDIENTS

8 ounces cream cheese, softened at room temperature

½ stick unsalted butter, softened at room temperature

2 tablespoons powdered sugar, sifted

¼ cup homemade mango-habanero jam (or use your favorite jam)

Tools: small bowl, electric beater, rubber spatula, plastic wrap

DIRECTIONS

Beat the butter and cream cheese together in a small bowl.

Add the powdered sugar and incorporate well.

Add the jam and beat till combined.

Wrap with plastic wrap as described above.

You can pipe this filling at room temperature and even immediately out of the fridge.

Note: This cream cheese and butter recipe also works well with vanilla extract. Instead of adding jam, use ¼ to ½ teaspoon of pure vanilla extract.

PAULA'S FAVORITE COMBINATIONS

The flavor combinations for macaron discs and fillings are too many to list. You will have to experiment to find the ones you like. Here are my favorite fillings with plain almond macs:

Dark chocolate ganache with coconut mixed in

Mango-habanero cream cheese filling with Himalayan pink salt sprinkled on the macs

Lemon curd filling with Himalayan pink salt sprinkled on the macs

Pistachio and almond paste filling

ABOUT PAULAQ and CLOSING

I have been a "pastry-chef-at-heart" since my years at the University of Oregon. Though I majored in exercise science, I rewarded myself with books such as Bo Friberg's The Professional Pastry Chef when I passed a college exam with a grade of at least 90 percent. I first fell in love with the art and science of beautiful, expensive sweets while enjoying the desserts at Excelsior Inn and Ristorante in Eugene, Oregon, from the early to the mid 1990s. The cute little place was a stone's throw from my college apartment.

I enjoy the attention to detail involved in cake decorating. I decorated a cake or two in high school and college, but most of my cake ventures were out of my Army housing quarters in Germany. I also worked for the local base commissary as its cake decorator. While in Germany at the end of the 1990s, I spent countless hours visiting bookstores of the many post exchanges hoping to find good dessert books.

I'm an island girl, a native of Guam, and I have written two Guam cookbooks, A Taste of Guam and Remember Guam. Remember Guam won two Gourmand Cookbook Awards in 2009. Video demonstrations for my cookbook recipes, along with the recipes on my website, are presented on YouTube.com via my YouTube channel, ceps92. For more information about my two Guam cookbooks, go to paulaq.com and select the tab with the corresponding title of the cookbooks.

In 2010 I had the opportunity to learn to take pictures from my husband. Armed with some new skills, I visited bakeries, bought their sweet goods, and brought the subjects home to take their pictures. I published my pictures and a corresponding review of each bakery on Examiner.com.

No longer able to lift very heavy weights in the gym, or run sprints outside, making macarons proved to be the personal challenge I was looking for. I only intended to write my own recipe, but after so much research and so many trials, I saw an opportunity to fill the need for a stable and reproducible macaron recipe using basic meringue. Though I didn't expect to go 19 rounds with the batter, I learned a ton and am grateful for the experience.

I am currently working on a World War II historical romance novel, Conquered, based on Guam just before, during, and after World War II. The characters in this book portray locals as well as the men in the U.S. Marines, Army, Navy, and Coast Guard. It's been a work in progress since 2006. I have found that I can only write and research when I am in the mood. Otherwise, the words simply don't jive. With practically every paragraph I write, there is research involved. Thus, it is taking a long while to finish, but I am making good progress. I can guarantee that when the book is done, it will be as close to the period, setting, and events of WWII on Guam as anyone could write about. If you would like to keep abreast of my progress on the book, visit my site, paulaq.com, and select the tab labeled "Novel: Conquered."

When I'm not writing, working on a video, or creating a recipe, I train a few fitness clients, try to get to the gym for my own workouts, and keep busy as the COO, CFO, and CEO of the EQ-NC-Household, supporting my hardworking husband and my kids.

My husband, Ed, is my rock, my hero, my best friend. I was a college girl at the U of O and he was an Army soldier in Bosnia when we first started talking on the phone. We chatted for two weeks and decided we would get married; we didn't even know what the other person looked like. Two weeks after that, he sent me his ATM card; crazy guy! A couple of months later, we met for the first time at Sea-Tac Airport, one week before our wedding date in December 1996. As of this writing, we have been married 16 years and a few months. We have a 10-year old son, Carson, and a 9-year old daughter, Evalie. They are 14 months apart and I am so grateful that the tough years of teaching them respect, discipline, and hard work are finally paying off. Yes, we still have a long way to go, but it was a long wait to get to this point too.

I have loved the challenge of making perfect macarons. Thank you so much for purchasing this book. I hope you enjoy Macarons Math, Science, and Art, and find it a valuable resource. I will post my new adventures to macaron land on my website; select the "Macaron Book" tab at the top of the site. I am looking forward to trying more filling combinations and taking more pictures.

Feel free to contact me via pquinene@paulaq.com for any questions about my books. My motto has always been "dessert first!"

Esta Ki—that is "till later" in Chamorro, the native language of Guam.

PaulaQ

REFERENCES

Books and Publications

Brunner, Martin. (February 10, 2013). Taste of the Triangle: The Bakehouse and Café. Culinary Lessons at A Southern Season.

Corriher, Shirley O. Bakewise, The Hows and Whys of Successful Baking. Sribner, 2008.

Figoni, Paula. How Baking Works, Exploring the Fundamentals of Baking Science. 2nd ed. Wiley, 2008.

Torres, Jacques. Dessert Circus. Morrow, 1998.

Web Pages

Asselin, Marie. A Macaron Troubleshooting Guide: Useful Tips and Advice to Master the French Delicacy. December 16, 2011, http://foodnouveau.com/2011/12/destinations/europe/france/a-macaron-troubleshooting-guide-useful-tips-and-advice-to-master-the-french-delicacy/#ingredients-09-almond-meal-look-wet.

Ms. Humble. "Macaron 101: French Meringue." April 23, 2012, http://notsohumblepie.blogspot.com/2010/04/macarons-101-french-meringue.html.

Parks, Stella. "The Ten Commandments of Macarons." May 21, 2011, http://bravetart.com/blog/TheTenCommandments.

———. "Hollow Pursuits." September 30, 2012, http://bravetart.com/blog/HollowPursuits.

"Physical Properties of Base," City Collegiate, http://www.citycollegiate.com/acidbasesalt3.htm.

Tissue, Brian M. "Definition of Acids and Bases." 1997 to 2000, http://www.files.chem.vt.edu/chem-ed/courses/equil/acidbase/aciddefn.html.

RESOURCES

United Restaurant Equipment Company

2654 S. Saunders Street

Raleigh, NC 27603

(800) 662-7342

http://ureco.com/index.html

Purchased: professional baking pans

A Southern Season

University Mall

201 S. Estes Drive

Chapel Hill, NC 27514

Phone: (877) 929-7133

http://www.southernseason.com/

Purchased: almond flour, gel paste food coloring, edible glitter, almond paste, pistachio paste, mango-peach jam

Michael's Arts & Crafts

Purchased: piping bag, couplers, decorating tips

Amazon.com

Purchased: Demarle Silpat non-stick baking mats

Countrykitchensa.com

Purchased: powdered food coloring

Kohls.com

Purchased: baking stone, rubber spatulas

CPSIA information can be obtained
at www.ICGtesting.com
Printed in the USA
LVHW061547120620
657960LV00007B/553

9 780741 496133